AGAINST THE NIGHT, THE STARS

AGAINST THE NIGHT, THE STARS

THE SCIENCE FICTION OF ARTHUR C. CLARKE

JOHN HOLLOW

Ohio University Press
Athens, Ohio
London

Copyright © 1983, 1976 by John Hollow
Addendum: *The Songs of Distant Earth*
© Copyright 1987 by John Hollow
Originally published 1983 by Harcourt, Brace, and Jovanovich.
Ohio University Press edition published 1987.

Library of Congress Cataloging-in-Publication Data

Hollow, John.
Against the night, the stars.

Bibliography: p.
1. Clarke, Arthur Charles, 1917-   —Criticism and
interpretation. 2. Science fiction, English — History and criticism.
I. Title.
PR6005.L36Z69   1987   823'.914   86-23826
ISBN 0-8214-0862-3 (pbk.)

For my children:
John Patton, Elizabeth Lee, and Joseph Walter Hollow

A few ideas contained in this book are included in an essay of mine published in the *Southwest Review*, and in a series of taped lectures about science fiction that I made for the Everett/Edwards Cassette Curriculum. I should like very much to thank Margaret L. Hartley, editor of the first, and Richard E. Langford and Mary Jane Urban, president and vice president of the second, for their encouragement of my first efforts to write about popular literature.

I should also like to acknowledge the receipt of a small grant from the Ohio University Research Committee; it freed me from the obligations of one summer's teaching so that I might reread the science fiction of Arthur C. Clarke.

Contents

1

Against the Night ...

I think that people are re-reading [H. G.] Wells because they are tired of ever-more-minute dissections of neurotic egos, and worn-out repetitions of eternal triangles and tetrahedra. Wells saw as clearly as anyone into the secret places of the heart, but he also saw the universe, with all its infinite promise and peril.

Arthur C. Clarke, Introduction to H. G. Wells, *The Invisible Man* and *The War of the Worlds* (1962)

AN important thing to remember about the science fiction of Arthur C. Clarke, it seems to me, is that it was written by an Englishman. Although he now calls Sri Lanka home, Clarke was born in Minehead, Somerset (in 1917), and he is therefore, by nationality as well as by predilection, an inheritor of the tradition defined by H. G. Wells.

What I mean will perhaps be clearer if I say that when I read the science fiction of Robert A. Heinlein, who is not only an American but also an Annapolis graduate, I am reminded, not of any of H. G. Wells' very-nearly passive protagonists, but of boot camp, of the relationship between the promising young recruit and the battle-scarred old veteran. When I read the science fiction of Russian-born but New-York-bred Isaac Asimov, I am reminded, not of any of Wells' visions of future cities, but of the city dweller's constant fear of a breakdown, of the short circuit that can ruin a machine, a life, a whole culture. When I read the science fiction of American and Mid-western-born Ray Bradbury, I am reminded, not of Wells at all, but of my own Midwestern and bookish childhood, of cupola-topped Victorian houses and white picket fences, of adults insisting that there is a real world outside of books. When I read the science fiction of Arthur C. Clarke, however, I am reminded of England's shrine to its most important scientific formulation, of the matching statues of Charles Darwin and T. H. Huxley in Kensington's Natural History Museum. More than any of his equally well-known contemporaries, it seems to me, Clarke is the inheritor, not of Jules Verne's desperate attempts to show—by having some character name its parts—that Nature is controllable, or of Edgar Allan Poe's equally desperate attempts to gain some control of the subconscious by bodying forth its most awful horrors, but of the bleak evolutionary projections of H. G. Wells, Huxley's most famous pupil at the Kensington Normal School of Science.

I will go further. I will suggest that appreciation of Clarke's stories and novels might well begin by seeing them as having appeared, as do the stars at evening, against the dark background of the far future anticipated by Wells' best-known scientific romances.

Wells' best-known scientific romances can be not unfairly represented by the moment in *The Time Machine* when the time traveller, who has voyaged far into the future, stands on the deserted beach which is the epitome of our deserted planet and watches the passage of one of the inner planets eclipse the much closer but now weakened Sun. "The darkness grew apace," he says:

> a cold wind began to blow in freshening gusts from the east, and the showering white flakes in the air increased in number. From the edge of the sea came a ripple and whisper. Beyond these lifeless sounds the world was silent. Silent? It would be hard to convey the stillness of it. All the sounds of man, the bleating of sheep, the cries of birds, the hum of insects, the stir that makes the background of our lives—all that was over. As the darkness thickened, the eddying flakes grew more abundant, dancing before my eyes; and the cold of the air more intense. At last, one by one, swiftly, one after the other, the white peaks of the distant hills vanished into blackness. The breeze rose to a moaning wind. I saw the black central shadow of the eclipse sweeping towards me. In another moment the pale stars alone were visible. All else was rayless obscurity. The sky was absolutely black.

As the time traveller explains to his guests, after he has returned to his own time, what the far future has in store is not the completion of humanity's upward climb from the beast, not a civilization even more urbane than that represented by their late-Victorian dinner party, but the bleak truth that the human race itself must end. From the viewpoint of the aeons, the traveller insists, his face almost as pale as the front of his dress shirt, not only individuals but the species itself must—like the bubbles in their champagne—wink in the light and be gone.

What the time traveller discovers in the far future, to put it another way, is how very true is the answer to the ancient riddle of the sphinx. It is indeed the human race which, having

enjoyed a morning and a noon, still must suffer an evening to
its existence. When the traveller first arrives in the future, his
machine comes to a stop at the foot of a monument, "in shape
something like a winged sphinx." "It chanced that the face was
towards me," he says; "there was the faint shadow of a smile
on the lips. It was greatly weather-worn, and that imparted an
unpleasant suggestion of disease." When we come to reread
this scene, aware of how the novel ends, we realize that the
sense of disease is not misplaced; we imagine that the sphinx
seems to smile, not just because it knows that the human race
has degenerated into the childlike Eloi and the cannibalistic
Morlocks, but because it anticipates the final truth not discovered by the time traveller until he has voyaged even further
into the future: that even the Eloi and the Morlocks are
doomed. As I said, it is Man himself who, having begun on
four legs (not like a baby, but like a beast), and having enjoyed a noon of civilization, still must end in degeneracy and
death.

The Time Machine means to suggest a change in perspective. It wants to argue that the future will not be endless
progress, that the workings of time will be as hard on the race
as they are on the individual. The same change in perspective
is described, for that matter, in the final pages of another of
Wells' best-known scientific romances, The War of the Worlds.
There, the narrator, who has, as has Earth itself, just survived a Martian invasion, suddenly realizes that he can no
longer look out of his study window without remembering that
he has seen the countryside in flames; he cannot visit the
crowded streets of London without remembering that he has
seen the city devoid of life; he cannot hold his wife's hand
without remembering that he has counted her, as she him,
among the dead. He is unable any longer to look upon the
world unaware of his own certain and humanity's probable
demise.

The same change in perspective is produced by the experi-

ence of riding on the time machine itself. Night is seen to
follow day, not as we usually see it, as each taking twelve
hours, but as quickly as "the flapping of a black wing."

> I saw trees growing and changing like puffs of vapour,
> now brown, now green; they grew, spread, shivered, and
> passed away. I saw huge buildings rise up faint and fair,
> and pass like dreams. The whole surface of the earth
> seemed changed—melting and flowing under my eyes. . . .
> Presently I noted that the sun belt swayed up and down,
> from soltice to soltice, in a minute or less, and that con-
> sequently my pace was over a year a minute; and minute
> by minute the white snow flashed across the world, and
> vanished, and was followed by the bright, brief green of
> spring. . . . I saw great and splendid architecture rising
> about me, more massive than any buildings of our time,
> and yet, as it seemed, built of glimmer and mist.

As Arthur Clarke himself has said of this passage, riding on
the time machine is very like seeing the results of time-lapse
photography. If one took a picture every aeon, the surface of
the Earth itself would be seen to melt and flow. "The hills are
shadows," Clarke says, quoting Tennyson; "they flow / From
form to form, and nothing stands; / They melt like mist, the
solid lands, / Like clouds they shape themselves and go"
("Technology and the Limits of Knowledge," 1973).

Clarke might have prefaced his quotation from Tennyson
by pointing out that in 1834 Thomas Carlyle called for a
"time-annihilating hat" which would free us from the illusion
of time, would—by "relating endings to beginnings"—reveal
the whole universe to be "the star-domed city of God." By
1895, Clarke would then have been able to say, the time-
annihilating time machine could only reveal to Wells' time
traveller that the human race, its works, even the Earth itself
are as temporary as the mist, as insubstantial as dreams. It was

no longer any more believable that the universe is God's than that the sky is a starry dome.

In that scene when the time traveller stands there on that deserted beach, he sees "the black central shadow of the eclipse sweeping towards me." "In another moment," he says, "the pale stars alone were visible. All else was rayless obscurity. The sky was absolutely black."

Wells acknowledges, to put it another way, that in the case of an eclipse of the Sun by one of the inner planets, the stars would still be visible, even the "pale stars" of a far-off future in which the universe is closer to burning itself out. So intent is he on suggesting the final night, however, the time when the stars themselves will have winked and gone out, that he over-states: he says, ignoring the stars he has just mentioned, that the sky is "absolutely black." He probably means that the sky in between the stars is absolutely black, but he is so bent on hinting at the return of Darkness and Old Night that he forgets the stars he describes just two sentences earlier.

It is exactly the time between now and some such far-off death of the stars that the fiction of Arthur Clarke insists on. For him, Wells is the too-quick despairer, too ready to accept the analogy that as the day dies so must the universe.

In "The Long Twilight," the last chapter of his essay collection *Profiles of the Future* (1962), Clarke quotes a particularly Wellsian passage from Bertrand Russell to the effect

. . . that all the labours of the ages, all the devotion, all the inspiration, all the noonday brightness of human genius, are destined to extinction in the vast death of the solar system, and that the whole temple of Man's achievement must inevitably be buried beneath the debris of a universe in ruin—all these things, if not quite beyond dispute, are yet so nearly certain that no philosophy which rejects them can hope to stand.

To which Clarke, possibly under the influence of J. D.
Bernal's *The World, the Flesh, and the Devil* (1929), a book
whose power he has often acknowledged, answers that while
"this may be true," while the far-off future may indeed include
some such ultimate implication of the second law of thermodynamics, some such ultimate dissipation of energy and loss of
heat, "the ruin of the universe is so inconceivably far ahead
that it can never be any direct concern of our species." As
Bernal puts it, the "second law of thermodynamics" may "ultimately bring this universe to an inglorious close, may perhaps
always remain the final factor," but we are still "too close to
the birth of the universe to be certain about its death."

Clarke goes on to say that, because we are surrounded by
young stars that will take billions of years to age, we know
that our galaxy is in the "springtime of its life." Even those
beings who will have adapted to the "dully glowing stars" of
the galaxy's old age, he continues, will have before them, "not
the millions of years in which we measure the eras of geology,
nor the billions of years which span the past lives of the stars,
but years to be counted literally in the trillions." There will be
"time enough, in those endless aeons," he concludes, "to attempt all things, and to gather all knowledge."

No philosophy, in other words, which fails to allow us to
identify with those strange future beings, however unlike
humans they may be, no philosophy which fails to allow us the
hope that some intelligence someday may have attempted all
things and gathered all knowledge, can itself hope to stand. A
philosophy which fails to allow us such hope is, in its own
way, as limited in its assumptions about the possibilities inherent in nearly infinite time and nearly infinite space as is that of
Wells' "philosophical writer," the narrator of *The War of the
Worlds*, whose thought was entirely Earth-and-human-
centered before the coming of the Martians.

Moreover, and in a more limited sense, as Clarke is quick
to point out in various contexts, neither the death of our
planet nor even of our solar system necessarily means the

death of the race. In "Transience" (1949), for example, a story of his which is really more meditation than story, Earth is presented as it is in *The Time Machine*'s far-distant future: as a deserted beach. Even though "two long curving arms" of "something black and monstrous" are presented as eclipsing the stars, the "something" is immediately identified as a "dark nebula" and specifically located at "the frontiers of the solar system." In spite of their malevolent appearance, then, the curving arms of darkness do not represent anything nearly so final as the return of Old Night. In fact, because Clarke finishes his story by focusing on a time in the future when Earth has circled closer to the billions of stars in the center of our galaxy, "whole areas of the sky" are much more hopefully seen as "an unbroken blaze of light." It is clear from the story that, while humans have left the Earth, they have gone to the stars; they have escaped, at least for a while, the encompassing arms of oblivion.

According to Clarke, the writing of "Transience" was inspired by A. E. Housman's "Smooth Between Sea and Land," a poem about time's "effacing" wave, which he admits has haunted him and from which he took the title of his first novel, *Against the Fall of Night* (1953). Housman's poem is about the inability of "Adam's seed" to "build or write" anything that can survive the wavelike sweep of time; Clarke's story is a trio of scenes, a triptych, each panel of which shows the same beach, though at moments widely separated from each other in time. In Clarke's first scene, a child, a hominid, the representative of a race not yet far evolved, comes upon the sea, dimly realizing as he does so that it embodies a force far greater than anything his people have yet encountered. In the second scene, another child, this one the representative of humans who have evolved far enough to use machines, plays on the beach, confident as he does so, and as children always are, that there is no limit to tomorrows either for himself or for his world. In the third, which is set in the future, a child is

forced to leave the beach, as his people are forced to leave the
Earth, because the dark nebula at the edge of the solar system
represents a force far greater than anything they have met
before. We are left with the image of the beach, "Under the
level light of the sagging moon, beneath the myriad stars . . .
waiting for the end." The beach is "alone now," we are told,
as it was "at the beginning." "Only the waves would move,
and but for a little while, upon its golden sands." But our
penultimate sight is of the "last of the great ships" leaving
Earth for the stars.

Thomas D. Clareson has said of "Transience" that it is
"dominated by a note of sadness." And the third scene certainly does have a nostalgia for the planet on which humanity
was born. But the story is really more of a celebration:
whereas Housman laments that neither walls nor words can
hold back time's "bursting wave," Clarke celebrates the evolution of intelligence, the discovery of how to survive, on the
planet and then in outer space. There is no fourth scene in
Clarke's story, but the third includes by implication yet another child, this one on the beach of another world. The third
child is able to imagine himself, not on Earth at all, but on
worlds "very far from Earth."

All of which is to say that, while it is true that worlds must
die as must individual humans, still that is not necessarily
reason to disagree with the second child when he sees his future seeming to stretch endlessly before him. As Clarke's "The
Long Twilight" points out: in almost-endless time and almost-
endless space it is not yet clear that humanity will have to give
up its optimism. "If we last a tenth as long as the great reptiles
which we sometimes speak of disparagingly as one of Nature's
failures," he says in another essay ("Across the Sea of Stars,"
1959), "we will have time enough to make our mark on
countless worlds and suns." "It may be," he says in the Epilogue he wrote for the astronauts' *First on the Moon* (1970),
"that the old astrologers had the truth exactly reversed, when

they believed that the stars controlled the destinies of men.
The time may come when men control the destinies of stars."

Such optimism, of course, is difficult to sustain. As we shall
see, Clarke knows as well as anyone the difficulties involved.
But his fiction continues to argue, albeit sometimes somewhat
desperately, that, before our line or the cosmos ends, our
descendants will have traveled to the stars. As inevitably as
our ancestors crawled up out of the sea, he insists, our children will decide to sail the larger sea. Our life upon the land is
but a "pause," he says, "between one ocean and the next"
("Across the Sea of Stars").

In a story originally published as "Seeker of the Sphinx"
(1950), for example, a story that was later given the more
inevitable-sounding title "The Road to the Sea," Clarke presents a young artist who finds that he can no more refuse to
travel to the stars than he can refuse to grow up.

The possibilities of human fulfillment other than such
travel, for that matter, as this story sees things, are not many.
The young artist is in love, but his love is seen against such a
background of self-deception and cynicism that it is impossible
to view his feelings as anything but temporary infatuation.
The young artist and his rival both see the young woman, not
as she really is, but as the projection of their own expectations
and desires. And an old man warns both young men, not only
that their beloved will grow old, but also that everything will
not necessarily be settled on the day she decides between
them; she might change her mind. He even suggests that they
play a game of chess to see who gets her "first."

What the story presents, then, without in any way suggesting that they are atypical, is young lovers not fulfilled by love.
A little child, one as unromantic as baby sisters always are,
points out to the young artist that, painful as his love may
seem, he is easily able to refrain from killing himself. What she
is really saying, although neither she nor the young artist quite

realizes it, is that he must be living for something other than his beloved.

The thing in the story that really captures the vanity of Earthbound wishes is, however, the beautiful and deserted city of Shastar, to which the young artist comes after he has fled home and the frustrations of love. In an action presented as happening five thousand years before, a background against which we are to see the story of the young artist, two brothers, each representing large portions of the human race, are seen as they take leave of each other at the foot of the "Golden Sphinx" that overlooks the city. The one brother is to travel to the stars, the other to remain on Earth. As their conversation makes clear, however, both really want the same thing: to regain the Eden legend says was lost. The departing brother expects to find new Edens on new worlds; the stay-at-home wants to remain in Shastar, the Eden that humans have built.

When we are first shown the Golden Sphinx, we think it seems "utterly indifferent to all the passions of mankind." It just broods over the sea and the city, the one the symbol in the story of that which cannot be controlled, and the other the symbol of humanity's attempts to control its environment. But since the departing brother insists that "the future is built on the rubble of the past," that "wisdom lies in facing that fact, not in fighting it," and even the stay-at-home brother has to admit that the lure of change will probably force Shastar, the most wonderful city humans have ever built, to go "the way of Babylon and Carthage and New York," we are not surprised, when the young artist arrives at the deserted city five thousand years later, that he finds on the face of the still-brooding sphinx, not the mocking half-smile Wells' time traveller found on a similar face, but "the stains of Olympian tears," the result of "countless raindrops" having "coursed down those adamantine cheeks." Clarke's story does not mock the human desire to regain a lost Eden; it both sorrows over and celebrates the fact that humans seem always and everywhere to be leaving old gardens and seeking new ones.

This description of the human condition is epitomized in the story by the giant mural the young artist finds on a wall in Shastar. It depicts the storming of Troy, but is focused on the sad face of Helen, watching from the battlements. When the young artist tries to copy that face, he finds that he has painted instead the face of the woman he loves. He begins to realize that his beloved is, as was the model who sat for the mural artist so long before, just the momentary embodiment of "that beauty whose service is the purpose of life, and its sole justification." He begins to understand that neither the woman he thinks he loves nor the planet he was born on can fill what is a desire of infinite beauty, a "divine discontent" which—as Clarke says in "Across the Sea of Stars"—"is one more, and perhaps the greatest, of the gifts we inherited from the sea that rolls so restlessly around the world." That discontent will be, Clarke continues, "driving our descendants on toward myriad unimaginable goals when the sea is stilled forever, and Earth itself a fading legend lost among the stars."

The face of Helen is sad, perhaps because the pursuit of beauty is so destructive, certainly because happiness is even less permanent than life. Clarke uses the legendary face to lament the inability of humans to be content, the restlessness that makes for failed loves and deserted cities. But the story does not end in tears; it goes on to assert that only the stars seem likely to be able to address our desire for the infinite. "We will not exhaust the marvels of the physical universe until we have exhausted the whole Cosmos," Clarke says in *The Exploration of Space* (1951); "and that project is still, to say the least, satisfyingly remote, if indeed it is theoretically possible."

When the descendants of the people who left Earth five thousand years before return, as they do at the climax of the story, they have "not yet begun to exhaust" the "wonders" of the universe "or to tire of its mystery." "Can you imagine what it means to hang in space amid one of the great multiple systems, with colored suns blazing around you?" one of them

asks the young artist; "I've done that; and I've seen stars floating in rings of crimson fire, like your planet Saturn, but a
thousand times greater." There is a whole school of criticism,
says the spaceman, which argues that "real art couldn't have
existed before space travel."

Clarke's story does not claim so much as that, but it does
argue, as does Clarke's praise of Wells with which I headed
this chapter, that both life and art on Earth are near exhaus-
tion, are too caught up in "worn-out repetitions of eternal
triangles and tetrahedra," love affairs that are bound to seem
insufficient. It is time, as Clarke says Wells does, to confront
the universe, "with all its *infinite* promise and peril" (italics
mine).

In fact, lest the humans still on Earth be able to continue to
resist such a confrontation, the story has the returning humans
be responsible for a "Sigma Field," a space-spanning force
field, a side effect of which is the probable destruction of the
Earth. The point of the threat, of course, is the parallel with
the atomic bomb. Clarke's use of the parallel, however, is interesting. The Sigma Field is a sign, not of the human race's
self-destructive urge, as the atomic bomb is in so much science
fiction of the fifties, but of humanity's continued youthful confidence. "For all their knowledge," the story says of these space
explorers, "there was still a feeling of experimentation, even of
cheerful irresponsibility, about many of the things they did.
The Sigma Field itself was an example of this; they had made
a mistake, they did not seem to mind in the least, and they
were quite sure that sooner or later they would put things
right." Humanity at its best, Clarke seems to argue, will not be
afraid of the side effects of trying to control the infinite; only
worn-out men and women cannot build upon ruins, cannot
seek to answer their divine discontent among the stars, cannot
wipe away the tears as—like Milton's Adam and Eve—from
Eden they take their way.

The Sigma Field gives another form to the truth discovered
by Wells' time traveller. It may be that the future of life on this

planet will be made impossible, not by the inevitable devolu-
tions of either humans or the solar system, but by human
error. But the returning spacemen bring back to Earth the
hope that, while humanity's pursuit of the infinite may burn
our towers, it may also launch a thousand ships, all of them
in search of a beauty more than Helen's.

What humans must do, to put it another way, is to learn
from the wind-blown spiders the young artist encounters as he
is leaving Shastar. "Not knowing whither they would travel,
these tiny creatures had ventured forth into an abyss more
friendless and more fathomless than any he would face when
the time came to say farewell to Earth." For Clarke, while the
evolution from land to space "will be the deliberate product of
will and intelligence," as opposed to the evolution from sea to
land which "was achieved by blind biological forces"
("Across the Sea of Stars"), still the urge to go into space is so
strong, so obvious, that it too may be spoken of as being
beyond control.

> Every civilization is like a surf rider, carried forward on
> the crest of a wave. The wave bearing us has scarcely
> started its run; those who thought it was already slacken-
> ing spoke centuries too soon. We are poised now, in the
> precarious but exhilarating balance that is the essence of
> real living, the antithesis of mere existence. Behind us lie
> the reefs we have already passed; beneath us the great
> wave, as yet barely flecked with foam, humps its back
> still higher from the sea ["Rocket to the Renaissance,"
> 1962].

But Clarke's response to Wells' legacy can perhaps best be
presented by comparing two of their stories, both of which
happen to be entitled "The Star" (Wells, 1897; Clarke,
1955). Clarke's story does not seem, at least not consciously,

to have been meant to allude to that of his predecessor, but both refer to the Star of Bethlehem, both contemplate the seemingly meaningless destruction of a civilization, and both finally are about whether the universe can be understood.

In Wells' story, a planetoid wanders into our solar system, where it collides with Neptune and ignites into a giant fireball, the new "star" of the title. As these interlocked bodies narrowly miss the Earth on their fall into the Sun, the result on our planet is terrible storms, earthquakes, and a flood almost as universal as that described in Genesis.

The theme is typically Wellsian: we humans, who thought ourselves the center of creation, suddenly realize that we are no more guaranteed survival than was Neptune. Our fate, for that matter, would be no more detectable over the vast distances of space than was that of whatever beings may have lived on that planet. A new star in the heavens, says the story, is much more likely to announce that the universe is a random and uncaring place than that a savior is born.

Clarke's story, in turn, is equally anti-Christian. A Jesuit priest, an astrophysicist, is returning to Earth from an expedition to investigate the remains of a supernova at the extreme edge of our galaxy. The investigators have found, buried on the planet which must have been the Pluto of the destroyed system, a time fault filled with the relics of a brilliant and beautiful civilization, destroyed when the star exploded. "It is one thing for a race to fail and die, as nations and cultures have done on Earth," the Jesuit says to himself; "but to be destroyed so completely in the full flower of its achievement, leaving no survivors—how can that be reconciled with the mercy of God?"

"I know in what year the light of this colossal conflagration reached our Earth," he says. "I know how brilliantly the supernova whose corpse now dwindles behind our speeding ship once shown in terrestrial skies. I know how it must have blazed low in the east before sunrise, like a beacon in the oriental dawn." "What was the need to give these people to the fire," he cries out; was it "that the symbol of their passing might shine above Bethlehem?"

It is not the ruin of civilizations that undermines the priest's faith. As he says, he and several other members of the expedition have "seen the ruins of ancient civilizations on other worlds." To such routine disasters he is able to answer, as the voice from the whirlwind answers Job, that "God has no need to justify His actions to man. He who built the Universe can destroy it when He chooses." The priest's real difficulty is the same as that of the people in Wells' story: his religion has claimed too much. The human assumption that this world is the center of the cosmos, which is exemplified in both stories by the Star of the Magi, is bound sooner or later to come up against the fact of other inhabited planets; perhaps in very dramatic fashion. Are we to believe, asks Clarke's story, that God so loved this world that He destroyed another for it? It would be better, the priest is close to deciding, if the crucifix were to be seen as "an empty symbol," if humans were to admit that the Earth-centered view of the universe has difficulties which not even the great founder of his order, not even the far-seeing Loyola of the Rubens engraving, could foresee.

If the priest is to keep his intellectual honesty, he must do as the people in Wells' story do: he must give up the idea of divine favor. (It is even suggested, in Wells' story, that such a surrender would bring about a "new brotherhood" among men, would make of the world a more Christian place than Christianity managed to do.) The priest must realize that the state of human knowledge is as the ship's doctor describes it to him one day when the two of them are looking out from the ship's observation deck at the "stars and nebulae" swinging "in silent, endless arcs." "Well, Father," the doctor says, "it goes on forever and forever, and perhaps *something* made it. But how you can believe that something has a special interest in us and our miserable little world—that beats me." Or as Clarke has said in another context, in answer to the psalmist's

"What is man that Thou art mindful of him?": "What indeed?" ("Of Space and Spirit," 1959).

The priest has to learn to see all peoples, his own and those of the destroyed civilization, as the latter present themselves in one of the "visual records" they left in the time vault: as children playing on a beach. The image does not favor one people over another; instead, it captures, as it always has, the poignant beauty of mortality, especially of mortality seen against the magnificent immensity of the universe. Some cultures may be swept away, as in Housman's "Smooth Between Sea and Land"; some cultures may learn to sail the sea, as in Clarke's "Transience." The point is that both are beautiful. The passing of culture is no worse than the passing of a generation, than the passing of an individual. We must concentrate, as does the art of the destroyed civilization, on the moment of youth against the sweep of time, on the moment of intelligent life against the background of death. From such a viewpoint, focused on such an image, it still might be possible for the Jesuit to hope that such beauty—simply because it is beautiful —is *Ad Majorem Dei Gloriam*. The universe and the existence of life in it still may testify to the glory of a creator.

The difference between Wells' "The Star" and Clarke's "The Star" is this faint hope still available to the priest. In Wells' story, the master mathematician, who has been staying up night and day calculating the path of the new "star," finally stands at his window and says, as if to the new star: "You may kill me. . . . But I can hold you—and all of the universe for that matter—in the grip of this little brain." What he means, of course, is that he has the words and the numbers to describe the catastrophe that is about to happen. He is able to conclude that the Earth is not the center of a planned universe, that the human race "has lived in vain." He can only stare his doom in the face, comfort himself that he has understanding, and say bravely: "I would not change. Even now."

For Clarke, as we have seen, the issue is not—at least not yet—so clear. The priest's too limited view of the universe is undermined by the timing of the supernova, but Clarke's story does not suggest that the destroyed civilization lived in vain, nor does it conclude that the universe was not made by *something*. George Edgar Slusser has said that, "paradoxically, the hero's perception of cosmic indifference coincides with clear proof of the Christian religion—the Biblical account was correct after all, there was a Star of Bethlehem." I am fairly certain that the supernova is *not* supposed to be a "clear proof of the Christian religion," but I do think Slusser is correct when he describes the story's "final juxtaposition" as "that of a lyrically heightened voice brooding on the spectacle of universal indifference." And I am sure that the story wants the outcome of such brooding to be open-ended, not to be simply the Wellsian conclusion that the cosmos is a random as well as a deadly place. The universe may be indifferent—that is certainly one of the conclusions the priest could come to—but the story offers intelligent life and beauty as contrary suggestions, as aspects of existence which make total pessimism uncertain.

In that it reopens questions that Wells clearly thought were answered, Clarke's fiction echoes Olaf Stapledon's *Last and First Men* (1930), a book by which, as Sam Moskowitz was the first to notice, Clarke has been much influenced. At the end of his epic of future men, Stapledon has the last of his Last Men still wondering whether the universe has meaning, and being forced to conclude that the only certainty is that humanity has been beautiful.

Man was winged hopefully. He had in him to go further than this short flight, now ending. He proposed even that he should become the Flower of All Things, and that he should learn to be the All-Knowing, the All-Admiring. Instead, he is to be destroyed. . . . The music of the spheres passes over him, through him, and is not heard.

Yet it has used him. And now it uses his destruction. Great, and terrible, and very beautiful is the Whole; and for man the best is that the Whole should use him.

But does it really use him? Is the beauty of the Whole really enhanced by our agony? And is the Whole really beautiful? And what is beauty? Throughout all his existence man has been striving to hear the music of the spheres, and has seemed to himself once and again to catch some phrase of it, or even a hint of the whole form of it. Yet he can never be sure that he has truly heard it, nor even that there is any such perfect music at all to be heard. . . .

But one thing is certain. Man himself, at the very least, is music, a brave theme that makes music also of its vast accompaniment, its matrix of storms and stars.

Even this passage, however, with so much of which Clarke so obviously agrees, is too Wellsian for him, too overawed by the approach of night. Instead, Clarke uses a different analogy, one inspired by all those tomorrows and all those stars so easily ignored by Wells, Bertrand Russell, and even Olaf Stapledon. Clarke ends his novels with births to match deaths, sunrises to match sunsets, with the hope that there still may be—in spite of all the arguments to the contrary—some meaning to the fact that the stars stand out "against the fall of night."

2

Time's Arrow

AS I have said in the first chapter, the science
fiction of Arthur Clarke can be seen as having
defined itself both within and against the tradition established
by H. G. Wells. Before I can dramatize that act of artistic self-
definition, however, I have to show how very like the fiction of
Wells the fiction of Clarke can be. I have to show that in both
the onset of night can seem unrelieved, can seem a fitting
symbol of humanity's hopeless future.

For Clarke, as for Wells, the only reasonable view of the
universe is that bequeathed to us by nineteenth-century science, especially by the second law of thermodynamics and the
evidence of the fossils. If Clarke, as I have also said in the
first chapter, refuses to concern himself about the heat death
of the universe—which is the ultimate implication of the second law of thermodynamics—his stories nevertheless do have
an almost Wellsian obsession with the probable death of our
species—which is the ultimate implication of the fossil remains of other species. In this latter sense, Clarke's fiction
begins with a vision very nearly as bleak as that of Wells' best-
known scientific romances.

Take "Time's Arrow" (1952) for example. It opens with a character explaining entropy, which is to say that it opens with an explanation of the ultimate implication of the second law of thermodynamics. "Entropy is a measure of the heat distribution of the universe," he says. "At the beginning of time, when all energy was concentrated in the suns, entropy was a minimum. It will reach its maximum when everything's at a uniform temperature and the universe is dead." The story itself, which is about two scientists who manage to travel fifty million years into the past only to fall prey to a dinosaur, climaxes when the assistant to one of them kneels beside the just-uncovered fifty-million-year-old tracks of a dinosaur and discovers that they overtake what he recognizes to be the equally fossilized tire prints of his chief's jeep. What the story really cares about, in other words, is not the far-off heat death of the universe, but that much nearer time when, in spite of all of its science, humanity's footprints will be as fossilized as those of the dinosaurs. The story echoes, though it does not quote, Tennyson's question whether Man, "Who loved, who suffer'd countless ills, / Who battled for the True, the Just," will be in time, as are the dinosaurs, "blown about the desert dust," "seal'd within the iron hills." The story laments, as does Tennyson, that "From scarped cliff and quarried stone" Nature seems to cry, "A thousand types are gone; I care for nothing, all shall go."

The part of the story that really makes it Clarke's own is the dream the assistant scientist has. In it, as he is walking along a road that stretches in either direction as far as the eye can see, the assistant scientist comes upon a signpost, the arrow of which is broken and revolves in the wind. On one side it says: To the Future; on the other: To the Past. The meaning of the dream, as I understand it, is that while the fact of heat loss and the fact of fossils may give a direction to "time's arrow," to humanity the past and the future are, in the only important sense, the same. Just as there was a time when humanity was not, so there will be a time when humanity will not be. Even if we do not concern ourselves about the far-off heat death of the universe, we know only too well from the evidence of the fossils that species do end. In this not-quite-Wellsian story we do not have to see a sign of the eventual return of Darkness and Old Night to suspect that our kind too will pass.

Nor is it surprising, in this age of Spengler and Toynbee, that Clarke has on occasion wondered whether the rise and fall of species and of civilizations might not be as inevitable as the birth and death of individuals or the peak and troth of waves. It is difficult imagining any speculative human being not so wondering, at least since Gibbon. Isaac Asimov, for example, to cite another science-fiction writer, built a trilogy out of just such speculations; and he entertained the much more dubious idea that humans might one day be able to predict and control such wavelike movements of history.

Clarke stops well short of such optimism. In his early stories he wonders sadly whether intelligence and the civilizations that are evidence of it do not just come and go, now in this part of the universe and now in that. He assumes that such massive movements cannot be controlled, cannot even be tinkered with. "Encounter at Dawn" (1953) insists, as part of a general thesis, that there is "always a skull hidden behind Nature's most smiling face," that even Asimovian galaxy-wide empires are doomed to fall. In fact, so certain of this inevitability is the story that it does not feel the need to specify the nature of the "shadow" or the "mistakes" that are destroying the empire. All we know is that the explorers from the empire, who have just reached prehistoric Earth, are so saddened by the inevitable fate of their empire that they even envy their unfeeling robot explorer; they wish they could be as it is: "devoid of feelings or emotions, able to watch the fall of a leaf or the death agonies of a world with equal detachment."

Peter Brigg has said of "Encounter at Dawn" that it is about visitors from an advanced civilization being called home before they can bring primitive humanity to a "great leap forward," before they can, in the words of one of them, bring the human race "out of barbarism in a dozen generations." And it is about that. But it is also about how, "as she often must do in eternity," Nature repeats "one of her basic patterns." Not only are both the visitors and the Earthmen humanoid, not only does our planet remind them of their home world, not only does one of them refer casually to cultures reaching or going beyond the stage of cities, but the story itself completes a pattern. It reveals that the meeting between the extraterrestrial explorers and Earth's primitive hunter, which is its central incident, takes place on the fertile plain where, more than a thousand centuries later, the hunter's descendants will build the city known as Babylon; a name not without its own connotations of the end of empire. The primitive hunter's culture is experiencing a "dawn," we suddenly understand; and it will have to live through a noon and an evening as well. The difference between the rise and fall predicted here and that predicted in *The Time Machine* is that here there is the suggestion of a cyclical pattern, but the grim and all-knowing smile of the time traveller's sphinx is nonetheless appropriate.

Moreover, in that in Clarke's story the explorers do not even have time to explain the few tools they leave behind, in that the only thing they really succeed in arousing in the primitive hunter is "a sense of loss he was never to understand," the story says that such inevitable risings and fallings cannot even be mitigated. All that can be handed on from one dying civilization to another is what one generation can leave the next, the melancholy and apparently unjustified sense that life might have been different, that the cycle might have been escaped. "I wish I could warn you against the mistakes we have made," one of the explorers says to the hunter; but the story itself seems to feel that such warnings, even if they could be given and were heeded, are no more likely to prevent the fall of civilizations than is a parent's advice likely to keep the child from also having to die.

Whether the cycle of such risings and fallings can be escaped is, as we shall see, a version of the question Clarke keeps coming back to (because he is no more able than are the explorers to look on the fall of a leaf and the fall of a world with equal detachment). But his early stories are governed by this almost-Wellsian obsession with the end of empires and of species. "The Awakening" (1951) is about a man who awakens from thousands of years of self-induced hibernation to find that insects have inherited the Earth. It is a Wellsian awakening, even though it is not like the awakening in that author's *When the Sleeper Wakes*; Clarke's sleeper awakes to find that humanity was not the center of the universe, that our species has passed.

In "The Fires Within" (1949) humanity is again destroyed, this time by a race of beings who rise—demonlike—from the center of the Earth. In spite of this suggestion of maliciousness, the other race does not even suspect that we exist until it is too late. Their rising to the surface of the planet is just a part of their civilization's ordinary development, and the destruction of our civilization is as natural as the consuming of any exterior by the fires that rage within. As one of the other beings says, drawing the very likely conclusion from the ruins of our civilization, "It may be our turn next."

At the end of "The Possessed" (1952), two lovers, who happen to have observed the lemmings' seemingly insane migration, are careful to turn to each other and to the anticipation of their life together rather than contemplate the possible future of all species suggested by such degeneration and racial suicide. The lovers would rather be possessed by thoughts of each other than by the vision they have just had of the land itself seeming "alive," seeming to be "a dappled brown tide . . . seeking the sea."

For that matter, the possibility of racial suicide, of being "possessed" by "the fires within" ourselves, has moved Clarke, as it has moved many science-fiction writers, to write a few "after-the-bomb" stories. In "History Lesson" (1949), a Venusian culture examines the relics found on a bomb-decimated Earth; and in "If I Forget Thee, Oh Earth . . ."

(1951), colonists on the Moon look back at an Earth gleaming with "the radioactive aftermath of Armageddon." But probably Clarke's most representative treatment of the theme is "The Curse" (1953), a meditation in which he focuses on Shakespeare's grave as a way of finding an image for an Earth destroyed by hydrogen bombs. He concludes with a closeup of the poet's epitaph, still readable although both the church and the town have been blasted out of existence.

> Good frend for Iesvs sake forbeare,
> To digg the dvst encloased heare;
>   Blest be ye man yt spares thes stones,
> And cvrst be he yt moves my bones.

As the river Avon, whose course has been changed by the blast, flows over the gravestone, we suddenly realize that the verses both assume and address future generations. The hope that one's bones will not be disturbed implies a continuing civilization, one that may have need of more space, if only to bury its dead. Suddenly we see that Shakespeare's curse has been made irrelevant in a way the bard did not imagine: no one now will move his bones.

I say that "The Curse" is representative of Clarke's handling of the "after-the-bomb" theme because, interestingly enough, the atomic catastrophe does not seem to have held any more terrors for the Clarke of the early stories than did various other potential catastrophes he could name and did write stories about; the Sun becoming a nova, for example, or the coming of another ice age. It is uncertain in "The Curse" —and finally does not matter—from whence came the particular bomb that destroyed Stratford. The bombs are pictured as falling back from outer space on an Earth they can "harm no more"; they are "falling at random," almost as if from a force as impersonal as Nature. We are told that the "blooms" of "indescribable flame," which are a result of the meeting of missiles high above the planet, will send "out into space a message that in centuries to come other eyes than Man's [will] see and understand." Atomic self-destruction becomes as natural as a nova.

The same observation might be occasioned by the final scene in another story, "The Second Dawn" (1951). A culture that has just avoided one sort of racial suicide, a self-destruction based on the extraordinary development of its powers of mental telepathy, will, we come to realize, be threatened in the future by a self-destruction based upon its just-beginning development of technology (the "second dawn" of the title). At the end of the story the culture reaches a moment that reminds us of our own Madame Curie; one of its females finds that she cannot take her eyes from the "enigmatic glow" given off by a rock her race has just discovered. We understand that the future threat may be avoided, as was the recent one, but the point is that such threats of racial self-destruction are as inevitable and as natural as the coming of noon or of night.

And so, although people would prefer not to think about it and would prefer to turn to each other as do the lovers in "The Possessed," the possibility of a catastrophic conclusion to the human race is always there, forecast not only by the films of atomic clouds, but by every fossil, every exploding star that brightens in the heavens, every furrow left by the glaciers on the face of the Earth. In "The Forgotten Enemy" (1953), a former professor of English literature is the last man alive on an Earth destroyed, not by atomic warfare, but by the planet's passing into a belt of cosmic dust and thus into a new ice age. As he looks out on a snow-covered Bloomsbury, the professor, in spite of his former profession, seems unaware, perhaps because he was never a religious man, of the symbolism implicit in the fact that the dome of St. Paul's has collapsed under the weight of the snow. More important, he also seems unaware of the symbolism implicit in the fact that the smokestacks of the Battersea Power Station seem to have become "thin white ghosts against the night sky." The professor, we begin to understand, is like Wells' philosophical writer in the days before the coming of the Martians; he still believes in the power of humans to conquer Nature. The professor is convinced that the sounds he hears to the north are the sounds of humans using atomic weapons to blast away the snow and ice, but the sounds are those of the glaciers "returning in triumph to the lands they once possessed."

As the professor searches the radio dial, trying to hear again the music "once called immortal"—as he stands at the window shouting lines from his favorite poetry, as if the words could "break the spell" that has "gripped the world"—the Moon shines impartially on the dead city and on the rows of books he is trying to preserve. The professor's faith in the power of humanity is misplaced; he is a monk facing a dark age that will have no renaissance. Not even the atomic weapons in which humans took such great pride, and of which they had such fears, are enough to give the species power over Nature. If humans have forgotten their more ancient enemy in their fear of atomic self-destruction, at the end of this story the fate that has always hung over the race like "Damoclean icicles" falls. Long forgotten but always there, like the Nature they represent, the glaciers return.

3

The Lotus-Eaters

ACCORDING to Wells' *The Time Machine*, eight hundred thousand years from now, but still millions of years before the time traveller is to stand there on that deserted beach, the human race will already have degenerated into the childish Eloi and the cannibalistic Morlocks. The novel assumes that, just as the human race must have evolved from lower forms, so it is possible that it may deteriorate, that it may evolve in directions that are less than human.

The fear of such devolution is a particularly modern form of humanity's ancient fear of the beast within itself. At the end of Wells' *The Island of Dr. Moreau*, the narrator, who has gotten from his experience (as did Gulliver from his last island) a picture of humans as being more beastlike than they pretend, says: "I could not persuade myself that the men and women I met were not also another, still passably human, Beast People, animals half-wrought into the outward images of human souls; and that they would [not] presently begin to revert, to show first this bestial mark and then that."

In Clarke's early fiction the possibility of devolution, into the cowlike Eloi if not into the carnivorous Morlocks, is a theme even more obsessive than the possibility of a catastrophic end to the race. There is not much that humans can do, after all, at least at the present state of their technology, if the Sun does begin to show signs of being about to explode or if the Earth does pass into a belt of cosmic dust and thus into a new ice age. There is not much that humanity can do, for that matter, if our nature is such that we cannot avoid atomic self-destruction. Either alternative, destruction by an uncaring universe or destruction by an uncaring racial self, argues that humanity was just another of Nature's unlucky failures—a theme in which the young Clarke (unlike the young Wells) does not seem to have found continuing inspiration. Instead, Clarke seems to have begun to allow himself to assume that humanity will be spared such catastrophes (or at least to acknowledge that there is more material for fiction in so hoping). Under the influence of writers as different from each other as John W. Campbell, Olaf Stapledon, and Alfred, Lord Tennyson, he seems to have begun to find material for fiction in the danger implicit in survival itself, in the possibility of racial decadence that may be (as it is in *The Time Machine*) the result of humanity's very success at protecting itself from natural dangers, at controlling its environment.

Clarke's early fiction includes a few stories in which human beings are seen as quarrelsome, as always ready to settle scores with an atomic duel. In "History Lesson" the Venusians try to reconstruct the lost culture of Earth from a single cartoon film which is, typically, full of "incredibly violent conflict," and in which, also typically, the cartoon figures are not really harmed. The short film ends with an expanded view of the central character's face, but because they want to read into that face all of the emotions a destroyed culture might be expected to feel, the Venusians are unable to decide what emotions the face is meant to suggest—whether "rage, grief, defiance, resignation, or some other feeling." From within Earth's culture, however, we have to admit that Donald Duck's "characteristic expression of arrogant bad temper" is not an unfair caricature of beings who insist on playing at violence with the naïve assumption that they will not finally be hurt.

Similarly, "Exile of the Eons" (1950) ends with the un-hopeful supposition that if the two last men left alive were to meet on an Earth long dead and under a dying Sun, each of them exiled from his own time and thus more typically human, one of them would still be good, a Socrates banished to the far future, and one of them would still be evil, a Hitler fleeing from the consequences of his crimes. The good man, the story goes on to say, would, in spite of a life lived according to contrary principles, still have to resort to violence to destroy the evil. On a Wellsian last beach, in a universe in which humanity no longer exists, the two last men would still have to fight the human race's ancient self-defining and self-destroying struggle against itself.

Even less flattering is the picture of human nature given by a story such as "The Parasite" (1953). There, a man in the present has his mind invaded by a time-traveling future mind, the product of a culture in which "science has discovered everything, when there are no more worlds to be explored, when the stars have given up their secrets." The humans of that future seek "some release from their intolerable boredom . . . by sending back their minds to an earlier, more virile age, and becoming parasites on the emotions of others" (which is sort of a perverse twist on Stapledon's Last Men being able to speak to us in the present through one of our own).

The story has a certain neatness in that the character whose mind is invaded, one Connolly, has been all of his life a womanizer, "the eternal Don Juan, always seeking—always disappointed, because what he [seeks can] be found only in the cradle or the grave, but never between the two." Similarly, when the future mind has experienced vicariously Connolly's death, he is "satiated for the moment," but the story knows that it is "for the moment only."

The story is even neater in that Connolly's friend, Pearson, whose mind is the next to be taken over by the future mind, is more than just the doubter who thought the explanation for Connolly's behavior was a guilty conscience. Pearson too has a quality of which the future mind represents the final development. He has enjoyed watching Connolly all these years, the affairs and how they always came to nothing. He has never judged; he has just observed "with a bright-eyed, sympathetic interest" that can hardly be called "tolerance," since tolerance implies "the relaxation of standards" he has "never possessed."

The story hopes that the future mind is not the only truth about the future, "that he and his race are an isolated cancer in a still healthy universe," but it acknowledges that the restless need to escape from boredom and the voyeuristic joy of being the watcher are two of the strains in humanity. And it admits that if that mind is the human future, then "everything we've striven for is in vain"; then we are all like Connolly's latest girlfriend, the beautiful Maude, whose features are so twisted by "despair and anger" that she looks "like a figure from some Greek tragedy."

But Clarke's more usual attitude about the nature of human beings is given by a story such as "Breaking Strain" (1949). There, two men are again compared; this time one of them is "hard but brittle," and the other, although "soft and self-indulgent," is "subtle and complicated." It is the latter, of course, who does not break under the "strain" named in the title.

The plot is one of pulp fiction's favorites: two men, whose spaceship has been holed by a meteor, do not have oxygen enough to last both of them until they can make port. As the story itself points out, their situation is very like that of "two hungry Pacific Islanders in a lost canoe." The cannibalism in this case is metaphoric; one man must die so that the other may breathe.

As Clarke handles it, none of the escapes from such a predicament usually offered by pulp fiction, none of the ways of saving both men, will work. The men will not be able to invent a way to make more oxygen, nor will they be able to hail a passing cruiser. In fact, the chief moral issue, whether the men may decide that one of them must die, is not allowed to come up at all. The pulps usually pretend to raise such an issue, and usually avoid it by finding some way to save both men; in Clarke's story both men agree that one of them must die.

The situation in Clarke's story is more like that in much modern, Existentialist fiction: a sudden and desperate change from the ordinariness of everyday life reminds the men of the truth they have always wanted to ignore, that they are "under sentence of death," in a "condemned cell" awaiting "execution." The question becomes, as it does in a story by Camus or Sartre, how we are to live in a universe in which we can no longer ignore the certainty that we must die. The one man— the one with the strict rules of behavior, the neat categories, the confident sense of what is right or wrong—is surprised to find himself trying to commit murder. The other, the self-indulgent and yet complicated one, although he breaks down at first, is able, because of his life-long flexibility, to recover enough control of himself, not only to forgive the other, but to suggest that they still draw cards to see which one must die.

In the most important sense, then, the story is about the nature of this creature called human, this being who must live, aware of his own certain death and under the "fierce sun and unwinking stars" of an uncaring universe. The story concludes with the moment when the soft, self-indulgent, and yet subtle and complicated man looks down on the planet he has lived to reach. He is able to enjoy for a moment, not only his escape from death, but also his altruistic act, his willingness to share the risk of death. He knows that on some future day he will look back at this moment with self-doubt. "Altruism?" he will say. "Don't be a fool! You did it to bolster up your own good opinion of yourself—so much more important than anyone else's!" He even knows that others will speak of him in whispers, as the spaceman who allowed his partner to sacrifice himself. But for the moment we are given a picture of humans as self-indulgent but also self-doubting, as lucky to be alive but also capable of surprisingly disinterested action even under the immediate threat of death.

It may well have been under the immediate influence of John Campbell's well-known story "Twilight" (1934) that Clarke began to wonder whether the future of this fortunate but often remarkably generous species might not be the over-development of its potential for self-indulgence. Near the end of *The Time Machine*, after the death of Weena and after his penultimate escape from the Morlocks, the time traveller decides that the human beings of the far future have divided into two races, the keepers and the kept. More to my point, he also decides that this future decadence has been brought about by the invention and perfection of machinery. Freed of the necessity of striving, he concludes, humans have slipped back down the ladder of evolution, becoming again children, even beasts. In John Campbell's version of this same unhappy future, which he puts into the mouth of another time traveler, the world of the far future is a world of towering cities, all run by machines and almost all totally deserted by humans. Like Wells' Eloi, Campbell's "little misshapen men with huge heads" have become again little children. Like the Eloi, Campbell's future people are interested for a moment in the strangeness of a time traveler in their midst, but they are soon distracted and wander off.

In "The Lion of Comarre" (1949), Clarke has the people of a much nearer future (circa the year 3000) be almost as undermined by the success of machinery. In a world of tower cities and "automatic farms," when machines themselves "seem as natural as the dawn," Clarke's future humans have turned away from science and its contemplation of the universe to the much more limited fields of statesmanship and a technically brilliant but unoriginal art. The story is about a young rebel who wants to make a career of science, even though his father is a famous artist and his grandfather one of Earth's governors. ("I don't think I'd mind so much," says the father, protesting his son's choice of career, "if you were content to do nothing, so long as you did it gracefully. Certain people excel at that, and on the whole they make the world more interesting.")

The story has a contrast between humans and animals ("Only animals are contented," says the would-be scientist). The juxtaposition becomes clear the moment the young protagonist visits Scientia, the island tower of the world's still-remaining scientists. As he steps out of his flyer, he is aware of the boom of the waves on the island's rocks, "a sound that [has] never failed to impress him." At the same time, against the background of that symbol of time passing and of destruction, he is also aware of the circling gulls and migrant birds that have "used this speck of land as a resting place" since before the time "when man was still watching the dawn with puzzled eyes and wondering if it was a god." It is this latter contrast, between animals, which do not change, and humans, who do, which argues that humans will not remain satisfied by a machine-run utopia.

Certainly, at the beginning of the story, when we visit the studio of the protagonist's father, we are supposed to begin to wonder if a new direction is not called for. If a thousand years from now sculpture is still a matter of turning "rough-hewn cubes" into "the shapes of animals, human beings, and abstract solids [to which] no geometrician would [dare] to give a name"—if people are still trying to sculpt animals, themselves, and the unreal shapes of their own minds—then we are surely to have a bit of the "weariness and disillusion" the protagonist feels when he looks upon the technically brilliant but decadent art of Comarre itself, of the escapist refuge which is the opposite of Scientia.

Similarly, when we visit the "artificial moon" which houses the World Council, we become aware of a double symbolism to the Council Chamber's "crystallite" roof. Through it may be seen "the great globe spinning far below"; and while it is surely true that no "narrow parochial viewpoint" about Earth's affairs is possible from that perspective, at the same time we are aware that "the great crescent of Earth" blots out the stars, that the Council has limited its attention instead to the starlike lights of the cities which dot the land below. We become aware, as does finally the protagonist's grandfather who heads the World Council, that the old men who run the planet are clinging to an unchanging culture the way they would like to cling to their lives.

It is this attempt to arrest change that characterizes Clarke's idea of the decadence humans may fall prey to. Wells' Morlocks and Eloi are the logical extension of the nineteenth-century's two classes, the workers and the worked for. Campbell's childlike future people are the logical extension of a patrician refusal to try to understand machinery. But Clarke's future decadents are the extension of humanity's far-older urge to control life, to escape from the implications of change.

The image Clarke uses for such an escape is borrowed, not from Wells or Campbell, but from Tennyson. It is a lotus, and it comes from Tennyson's "The Lotos-Eaters." In that poem, Odysseus' worn-out warriors ask: "Ah, why / Should life all labour be? . . . Is there any peace / In ever climbing up the climbing wave?" As Clarke's decadents put it: "The aim of all life is pleasure and the pursuit of happiness. Man has earned the right to that. We are tired of this unending struggle for knowledge and the blind desire to bridge the stars."

In Tennyson's poem the mariners who have tasted of the lotus "muse and brood and live again in memory / With those old faces of our infancy / Heap'd over with a mound of grass, / Two handfuls of white dust, shut in an urn of brass." Under the influence of the drug, the world becomes a place in which it seems "always afternoon"; where "the slender stream /

Along the cliff to fall and pause and fall did seem"; where the choice is not just "long rest or death, dark death," but also "dreamful ease." In that latter state, because the mariners can live as if their dream were the only truth, both death and time seem conquered; the mariners can "live and lie reclined / On the hills like Gods together, careless of mankind."

In Clarke's story such decadence is found in the tower of Comarre, in the dream machine which feeds the mind with images so real-seeming that the sleepers cannot tell the difference. The "curse of Adam" seems "lifted" in Comarre, not just in the sense that machines now do the work of people, but also in the sense that the immortal life of our first parents seems regained.

Such an escape cannot last, as least not for the protagonist; it is too life-denying. The young man is awakened by a call on his radio receiver, by the demands of his culture, and he resolves never to sleep again in Comarre. The attractions of such a dream world are testified to, however—as they are in another Tennyson poem, "The Palace of Art"—by having the young man wonder whether he may not one day yearn to return to the pleasant illusions.

Be that as it may (and the story does not tell us whether the young man will eventually find reality so unrewarding), the decadence Clarke's protagonist escapes is not just a return to the beast or a surrender to the ease of a machine-run utopia. In fact, the "lion" of "The Lion of Comarre" is both the old man, now long dead, who built Comarre but was too much involved in the pursuit of knowledge to succumb to its enticements, and the real lion which—doglike—follows the protagonist into Comarre and, at an important moment in the story, protects him by attacking the robot representative of the central machine. The old man as lion argues that the best part of the human race will continue to find the attractions of knowledge more compelling than the attractions of escape; the real lion's attack on the robot argues that humanity will continue to dominate the machine, in part because of the beast which we are more than, but which still lives within us.

At the end of the story, the protagonist, having received from the central machine all of the notes of Comarre's builder, falls asleep (but does not dream). He has the lion at his side and his face toward the stars. The taking of the notes out into the world says that the breaking down of "the barrier between Man and Machine"—which Comarre, even at its worst, represents—is also the way to more knowledge, to the stars. As Mary S. Weinkauf has pointed out, the escape from Comarre is in fact an escape from the Garden of Eden. The decadence avoided, one might say then, is the decadence of the unfed imagination, of a refusal to leave an Earth that can be made Edenic; it is the attempt to forget the taste of the Tree of Knowledge.

The decadence of future human beings is explained in Clarke's first novel, *Against the Fall of Night* (1948), not so much by the triumph of machinery, as by the human fear of the dark and of all it can be made to represent. Far in the future, on an Earth whose seas have long since gone dry, a remnant of humanity has retired into the self-contained and machine-run city of Diaspar. They have turned their backs on the desert the rest of the planet has become, and they use the city's lights to keep themselves from being aware of the desert places suggested (as in Frost's "Desert Places") by the distances between the stars. They have gathered together all of the treasures of the race, "everything that has been saved from the ruin of the past," and they have made themselves and their city nearly immortal in the hope that Diaspar will "live and bear the descendants of Man safely down the stream of Time."

If anything, the citizens of Diaspar are too aware that their city one day will end, that the Earth itself will pass away. They try desperately not to remember that "of the oceans, nothing [remains] but the grey deserts of salt, the winding sheets of Earth." They have to concentrate on the joys of their city to forget that the rest of the planet is "salt and sand, from Pole to Pole, with only the lights of Diaspar burning in the wilderness that must one day overwhelm them."

When the "leagues of blue water, greater than the land itself, [rolled] their waves against the golden shores," at least travel was possible; if the "boom of breakers" reminded humans that nothing lasts, the oceans at least invited men and women to see more, reminded them that humanity had learned to ride the surface of one destructive element. In the far future, all that is left is the sense of "the desert lapping round the island that [is] Diaspar."

The novel itself travels from ruin to ruin. It starts with the overall view of our planet turned desert; visits the tomb of Yarlan Zey, a memorial to one of the city's designers; inspects the rubble of Shalmirane, according to legend the site of humanity's last battle with the Invaders, who are said to have driven them back to Earth from space; and climaxes on another planet, in the "utter silence" of the Central Sun's giant world, once the center of a galactic empire, now completely deserted.

Each of these ruins, however, like the ruins of classical Greece and Rome out of which our own Renaissance may be said to have grown, implies the greatness of humanity; reminds Alvin, the novel's young protagonist, that what humans once were they might be again. Beneath the great flagstone at which the statue of Yarlan Zey seems to stare, Alvin finds Earth's long-deserted underground transportation system, the many tunnels of which suggest the many alternatives to the decadent "prison of Diaspar." Amidst the ruins of Shalmirane, he comes upon the last apostle of the Master, the long dead teacher whose gospel of the "Great Ones," it turns out, also apotheosizes the human race. And on the planet of the Central Sun, just as he is about to agree that Diaspar has been right all along to fear that all roads "lead" but to "ruined cities," he is reached by

Vanamonde, the "pure mentality" once created by humanity in the hope that something someday might come closer to understanding the universe.

The novel is also organized, appropriately enough for a story about the recovery of past glories, as an inquiry into the truth about the past. Rather neatly, Clarke has humanity's greatest achievements already having happened; the novel is able to create the certainty that the great claims it makes for humanity, which a more traditional novel would set in the future, are true: they take on the certainty of history.

The past which Alvin's inquiries recover, and which destroys the myth of the Invaders, is the story of humanity's first attempts in space and of the meeting there with intelligences far greater than its own; the story of the Wellsian discovery that we are not the center of the universe.

It is also the story of Man's coping with this discovery, of his decision to return to his own planet and "to drive himself to the limits of his evolution." It is this taking over of the direction of evolution that the novel offers as a hope that humans may still have an important part to play in the history of the cosmos, even though they are not as important as they once thought they were. When Alvin looks to the past, he discovers there, not the fact of evolution (that is a given), but the fact that the race has improved itself, that it once controlled the direction of change (in an experiment that "consumed the entire energies of the race for millions of years").

It may be, as Sam Moskowitz has suggested and Clarke has to a certain extent agreed (in the Introduction to the 1968 reprint of the novel), that *Against the Fall of Night* was inspired by the long vistas of years in Olaf Stapledon's epic chronicle of future history, *Last and First Men*. (Clarke also credits John Campbell's "Twilight," Debussy's *L'Après-midi*, and his own "transplantation" from Somerset to London.) But Stapledon's long saga ends tragically; it is a description of the changes evolution rings upon the human race before the Last Men pass from existence. If one copies, as Clarke says he remembers doing, Stapledon's "Time Scales," one cannot avoid noticing that on the last one, as Clarke puts it, " 'Planets Formed' and 'End of Man' lie only a fraction of an inch on either side of the moment marked 'Today.' " To get something like Clarke's positive hopes for evolution, one has to look at the tradition Stapledon was probably reacting against (as was Wells): the tradition that may be defined by Tennyson's *In Memoriam*. At the end of that very Victorian and very English epic elegy, the "far-off divine event, / To which the whole creation moves" is the evolution of the human race into God.

Be that as it may, Alvin discovers that in the distant past the human race, much evolved, having become long-lived and telepathic, returned to space to play an important part in the creation of a galactic empire. After billions of years, however, having discovered from contact with other species "how profoundly a race's world-picture" depends "upon its physical body and the sense organs with which it [is] equipped," humans decided to take over evolution again, to create a "pure mentality," a mind "free from such physical limitations."

The result of that "great experiment," unfortunately, was "the Mad Mind," a pure mentality "either insane or . . . implacably hostile to matter," which had to be brought under control and bound "by forces [of] which we cannot guess," by forces that left the whole galaxy "dimmed" as if the "stars themselves" had been "drained of their power."

As a side effect, the failure of this great experiment drove some humans back to Earth, away from the stars (thus creating the legend of the Invaders). These gave up the attempt to create beings who might one day better understand the universe; instead, they built the city of Diaspar, within the walls of which they could control almost everything.

Fearful as had been the failure of the great experiment, other humans resolved to try again. This time they succeeded; this time they created Vanamonde. But the creature is less important to the novel than is the fact of trying again. Vanamonde is just the extension of the human desire to understand the universe, but the decision to try again is a refusal to give up, is a refusal to agree that the passing of the human race is a foregone conclusion. Against the retreat into Diaspar, against all of the uncontrollable forces suggested by "the fall of night," the novel offers a reaching for the stars. The stars become not so much a destination as a sheer sense of numbers, of alternatives. The stars offer a near-infinity of possibilities to match the more-nearly-infinite darkness which cannot be controlled.

Diaspar itself, the beautiful human-created ornament on the bosom of the desert, is testimony to humanity's ability to control much, if it cannot control all. So too are the machines that run the city. But the strongest statement of human power, limited as that power may be, is the deathbed utterance of that celebrator of humanity, the Master—the one bit of his gospel that has come down through the millions of years ungarbled: "It is lovely to watch the colored shadows on the planets of eternal light," he said; and just as Vanamonde is in a way the reality dreamt of by many "very ancient religions," so the Master's dying statement has a truth that Alvin can only appreciate after he has recovered the Master's starship and visited the constellation known as the Seven Suns. Alvin had wondered whether the perfect circle of six suns around a white central sun, "one for each of the primary colors," could be natural; when he gets there he realizes that intelligence must have built the system, that it is a triumph of science and art, that "its superb symmetry [is] a deliberate challenge to the stars scattered aimlessly around it." It is lovely to watch the colored shadows on the planets of eternal light because on a planet surrounded by seven suns there can never be any darkness, and because the system itself is intelligence's greatest attempt (before Vanamonde) to address the uncontrollable.

The thing wrong with Diaspar, then, is not that it attempts to control the uncontrollable; it is that the Diasparians have reduced the scope of human life to that which *can* be con-

trolled. They have become old and afraid of change. Like
most immortals or near-immortals in folklore and literature,
they have continued to live without being able to continue to
be young. Like Tennyson's "Tithonus," they are being consumed by immortality.

Alvin, on the other hand, is the most recent embodiment of
the spirit of youth. He is the first child born to the near-
immortals of Diaspar in over seven thousand years. He is
curious, unafraid, persistent, and self-concerned as only youth
can be. He acts on impulse, and in that sense the book is about
his growing up, about his discovery that the changes and evolution he wants for Diaspar are as natural as growing up.

Alvin manages to succeed in freeing Diaspar from its stag-
nant state because he is in tune with the nature of things.
Thomas D. Clareson has argued that, whereas "Alvin largely
controls the action of the first half of the story," from that
point onward "he is manipulated by his discoveries." But such
is exactly the point. Even though it seems at first that, as
Clarke puts it, the "long, slow decline of human will" is "too
far advanced to be checked by an individual genius, however
brilliant," Alvin is able to move his people, to become a great
man driving them, because he identifies with the flow of
events, with change rather than staying the same. Like all
great men, Alvin happens to be going the way of history.

Alvin's first discovery is that "there is a better way" of leaving Diaspar than the long climb down from the towers to the
desert floor. He discovers that although the seated statue of
Yarlan Zey is examining the plans spread across its knees, the
plans are not those of Diaspar; the figure is staring at the
flagstone that conceals the subway out of the city, and the
plans are the plans of the city's founders to allow the possibility of change in Diaspar. The "better way" turns out to be to
live with change, not to try to prevent it.

Alvin creates a "vortex" into which the other characters
feel themselves dragged because he is young and innocent

enough to entrust himself to the flow of events. He is able to enter into the underground train, into the arms of the Master's robot, and ultimately into the Master's starship—all of which lead him to the truth about evolution in the past, and thus to his understanding that change is better than the absence of change, his understanding that evolution is a force which humans (with the help of their machines) may be able to ride.

It is interesting to note, in this regard, that the cover of the issue of *Startling Stories* (November 1948), in which *Against the Fall of Night* was first published, illustrates the moment when Alvin entrusts himself to the arms of the Master's robot. Not only is the woman in the picture a good deal less clad than anything the story suggests, but the robot becomes the mad machine of pulp fiction and Alvin himself its unwilling victim. But such is exactly the cliché against which Clarke was working; in this novel the machine is not the cause of human decadence, it is humanity's ally against the dark, its means of passage to places other than despair (Diaspar).

One of Alvin's first discoveries is that there still exists on Earth a colony of humans better able to be in this somewhat frightening universe than are the citizens of Diaspar. In the rural village of Lys (so called it seems because they too believe the lie about the Invaders) live men and women who have not turned their backs on Nature, who have given up immortality in order that youth might not pass from their culture. (A "world which [banishes] death must also banish birth," says one of their rulers, referring, it would seem, not just to the lack of resources but to the control of change. The "power to extend his life indefinitely brought contentment to the individual," she goes on, "but stagnation to the race.")

Alvin wants to bring the people of the city and the country back together, in part because he thinks the citizens of Lys do not live long enough, that they could extend their lives at least a little longer as a result of the reunion with Diaspar, but chiefly so that the whole race will regain the youthful willing-

ness to live between that which can be controlled and that
which cannot, between that which is man-made and that
which is natural.

In the last scene of the novel, Alvin stops the Master's starship above one of Earth's poles. As he looks down upon "the
belt of twilight," he realizes that he is "seeing at one instant
both sunrise and sunset on opposite sides of the world." The
"symbolism," he decides, is both "perfect" and "striking." In
this galaxy, he suddenly understands, night is falling. But elsewhere the stars are "still young" and "the light of morning"
still lingers. And *along the path he once had followed, Man
would one day go again"* (Clarke's italics).

George Edgar Slusser has said of this novel that each successive stage of Alvin's journey "ends with a spectacle of
human passing that he is powerless to change." But in fact
each successive fall of night is followed by a morning. Alvin
turns out to have much power to change things, exactly because he identifies with—even subjects himself to—the natural rhythm of sunset and sunrise. He finds it to be at least
as symbolic as is the more pessimistic reading of sunrise to
sunset.

In the past, humanity met intelligences far greater than itself out among the stars, and so it returned home to Earth to
be born again, to evolve into the best the race could be. Humanity tried to create a pure mentality, failed, and yet tried
again. And humanity, we find out, the Great Ones of the
Master's predictions, also left this galaxy. After the creation of
Vanamonde, some humans made the "first contacts with a
very great and very strange civilization around the curve of the
Cosmos. This civilization, if the hints . . . are correct, had
evolved on the purely physical plane further than had been
believed possible."

There are many possibilities, in other words, many reactions besides despair and lies to the threat that the race, like its
individuals, may die. In nearly infinite time and nearly infinite
space, it is not yet clear whether the human race may not be

able to evolve in its combination of the mental and the physical to heights as yet undreamed of. It may be, as one of Alvin's teachers believes, that in this galaxy the Mad Mind and Vanamonde must ultimately meet. It is also probable that that is a future "in which Man [will] play no part." But there are other galaxies and other possibilities, and it is not yet clear whether in some of these we may not have a role. The only evidence is the evidence of the past, and that evidence seems to argue that there is both continuation and change. The "path" of exploration and evolution is the path humanity has always followed; it can but follow it again.

The citizens of Lys, let me note in conclusion, have managed to keep their telepathic powers. The citizens of Diaspar, on the other hand, have not. The difference is, in part, the difference between the country and the city as Clarke perceived them after he left home for London—as our whole culture has perceived them, at least since Wordsworth. (The village has a better sense of community, we are often told; in the city, neighbors do not know each other.) But from the novel's point of view the more important reason the citizens of Lys still have their telepathic powers is that they still live for the whole—for their village and, by extension, for the race. They are, not to put too fine a point on it, willing to die so that the race may grow.

At the end of the novel, Alvin sends the Master's starship off to find the Great Ones. He knows that, long-lived as he is, he may not be here when and if they return. Even "if not," says the most important line in the novel, he is "well-content." He has done his part to free the race to grow. He is, as is the protagonist of "Breaking Strain," willing to die for the sake of his idea of what humans—at their best—can be. At one point in the novel Alvin looks at the ruin of another city and thinks that it is "heartbreaking" that "billions of men have left no other trace of their existence save these furrows in the sand." By the end of the book, he is willing to die for the sake of the future billions.

4

Prometheus

AT the end of "Rescue Party" (1946), Clarke's second published story, the crew of a survey ship from the Galactic Federation discovers that the human race, the youngest species in the galaxy, has managed to construct the largest fleet of spaceships on record.

In the story, Earth is about to be destroyed by the Sun's becoming a nova, and the survey ship has raced across millions of miles of space to try to save at least a few humans. What the would-be rescuers find is that the young race, which could not even be identified as intelligent the last time a Federation ship visited our solar system (a mere four hundred thousand years ago), has managed to save itself. The humans have "dared" to try to use "rockets to bridge interstellar space."

"You realize what this means," says the ship's first officer. "It would take centuries to reach the nearest star. The whole race must have embarked on this journey in the hope that its descendants would complete it generations later."

"You know," the captain replies, "I feel rather afraid of these people. Suppose they don't like our little Federation? . . .

After all, we only outnumber them about a thousand million to one."

The first officer laughs politely at what he takes to be his captain's little joke; but, "Twenty years afterwards," reads the last sentence of the story, "the remark did not seem funny."

Such optimism about the importance of the human race is not easy to maintain. As we have seen, Clarke's fiction is more optimistic than that of Wells; but *Against the Fall of Night*, for example, which was published just two years after "Rescue Party," ends with the much less extreme hope that the analogy of another dawn will prove to be truer about human affairs than is the analogy of a coming night.

In the novels he wrote just after World War II, however, *Prelude to Space* (1951), *The Sands of Mars* (1951), and *Islands in the Sky* (1952), Clarke insists that the human race is important, that it will increase its control over Nature, and that it may even discover the ultimate secrets of the universe. These novels say that the race will come to be, as Mary Shelley's irresponsible man-maker, Victor Frankenstein, did not, "the modern Prometheus." The race will prove capable, not of creating life in any new way, but of casting off the chains of its home planet and of carrying fire back to the heavens. These three novels of Clarke's are all versions of *Prometheus Unbound*.

Islands in the Sky is a boys' book. It is set in the near-future, aboard space stations that circle high above the Earth, is much concerned about hardware, and is among other things something of a guided tour of the stations. At the same time it is also held together by its assumption that humanity has the power to foster a positive attitude about existence by reperceiving the blue dome overhead, by seeing that the sky is an ocean.

The novel's teen-age protagonist, Roy Malcolm, on the evening before he leaves home for space, takes his homemade telescope out into the yard and scans the sky, looking for a space station, one of those artificial "stars" the human race has added to the heavens. He tries to imagine what it must be like, "up there in that floating bubble, with the emptiness of space all around." All he can experience, however, is the sight of the station passing into the Earth's shadow. Like Wells' time traveller, he cannot see beyond the fall of night.

At the close of his first day in space, on the other hand, Roy has a more positive experience. He is able to see, when he is taken outside of the space station in a spacesuit (his own little bubble of air and warmth), that the sunset resulting from the Earth passing between the station and the Sun is a glorious golden crescent which spans the planet. He is also able to see that the resulting darkness is so full of stars that he wonders "how anyone could ever have spoken of the 'blackness' of space."

We know from *Against the Fall of Night* that this scene can be read as a miniature of Clarke's fiction at its most hopeful. From the perspective of outer space, because even being there says that the race is continuing to grow, sunsets seem appropriately even more glorious than they do on Earth; they suggest that—when seen from the proper perspective—all conclusions (even deaths) are beautiful. Change at least is happening; stagnation is being avoided. Death is a contribution to the ongoing process; stagnation is a living death, changelessness.

Similarly, in space the observer can appreciate, as he never can on Earth, how stunningly the onset of night is matched by the revelation of the stars. The existence of other suns gives a reality to the hope that, lonely and silent as may seem the universe, the "blackness" of space is not the only truth.

Earlier in the same scene, when Roy first steps out of the space station, he is fearful of the five-hundred-mile fall beneath him. He is able to remind himself, however, as he has often tried to explain to his mother, that although space stations are falling, they are falling *around* the Earth. He is the beneficiary of humanity's study of centrifugal and centripetal force.

It is this ability of humans to control their falls—to make for themselves "floating bubbles" of light, heat, and air—that the novel celebrates. When Roy discovers that looking down on the Earth makes him giddy, he looks instead at the nearby space station; it is more encouraging. Some such reorientation is necessary in space, he says; and in the novel as a whole the escape from gravity is an escape from the ordinary way of seeing things. In space, sunsets and fears of long falls lead to contemplation, not of the death of individuals or even of the species, but of the race's continuing growth, its ongoing progress at control. When Roy looks at the still-growing space station, he sees its naked girders shimmering in the moonlight; they seem "the treads of a ghostly spider's web, a web sprinkled with myriads of stars." The silence and the loneliness of the universe, in other words, will force the mortals of any intelligent species to try to bridge the interstellar distances, to try to catch the nearly infinite promise of those other islands in the sky.

The power of humanity to reach for the only visible alternatives to the fall of night is represented in the novel by Commander Doyle, the space station's training officer. Doyle is a man who has spent all his life in the space effort, and he has been scarred by the process (he lost both legs on the first expedition to Mercury). But Doyle is also able to handle the two truly life-threatening moments in the book, the rescue of a silly movie star who gets himself into danger and of a whole shipload of young men whose ship is headed out into deep space and whose fall is no longer under control.

Doyle's loss of his legs makes two points for the novel. It reminds us that existence is dangerous, and it argues—conversely—that humans have nothing to fear in outer space that they have not met before. When Doyle tells the story of the first expedition to Mercury, and describes the Mercurians as having pincers, we leap to the conclusion that that is the way he lost his legs. But in fact the Mercurian used its pincer to throw a rock that broke the heating system in Doyle's suit; it was the unimaginable cold of Mercury's "dark side" that did the rest. Doyle lost his legs, not to any danger peculiar to Mercury, but just as any number of arctic explorers lost their extremities: through a failure of their particular bubbles of warmth.

Doyle is, then, the embodiment of humanity as explorer. His is the spirit which investigated the dark corners of this world long before the human race decided to visit the dark side of Mercury. When Roy Malcolm first sees him, the Commander is seated behind his desk, and he is described as being "the most powerfully built man" Roy has ever seen. His "huge arms" cover "most of the desk in front of him," and when he looks up, Roy is only aware of "staring at a huge red beard and two enormous eyebrows." The scene is a close echo of a similar meeting in Arthur Conan Doyle's *The Lost World*, when the young newspaperman meets Professor Challenger, the famous explorer, whose arms, eyebrows, and beard produce a similar effect, and that may explain Clarke's choice of Doyle as the name for the training officer. Like Challenger, Clarke's Doyle personifies humanity's challenge to the universe.

At the conclusion of Roy's flight up to the space station, the pilot asks him if he would have preferred a little more excitement, "a few meteors, an attack by pirates, an invasion from outer space, or all the other things you read about in the fiction magazines."

Roy answers that he does not read such magazines, but the pilot does not believe him and neither do we. Be that as it may, Clarke certainly read such magazines, and he uses pulp plots to repeat the novel's hope: that the human race may be more of a match for the universe than the analogy of sunset and death might suggest.

The novel's chapters break exactly as did the old serials.

Almost every chapter ends with some terrible threat, and the following chapter begins with the revelation that the threat was not as dangerous as it appeared or that the hero has up his sleeve some solution to the situation. Thus the holing of the space station by a meteor turns out to be a classroom exercise, a demonstration of standard operating procedure. And the monster from outer space turns out to be in fact from Earth, a hydra overgrown in the absence of gravity, a creature usually so small that it lives in ponds and can only be seen under a microscope.

Humans are unlikely to meet, in other words, anything on other planets more dangerous than they can find on Earth. Monsters can only kill, after all, and that threat is certainly common enough. Learning to avoid and, especially as a race, to survive such threats is what evolution is all about.

The giant hydra would be dangerous, explains a scientist, if its poison buds had not been neutralized. Each of the situations the characters get into in the novel could similarly be dangerous, were the power of humanity to neutralize the danger not sufficient. The climax of such neutralization is the moment when the boys look out the port of a spaceship and see a "slowly approaching missile" on the side of which is painted "the symbol of death—the skull and crossbones." The missile turns out to be a canister of radioactive waste, left over from the 1970s, and the boys' ability to leave it behind is symbolic of humanity's escape from that most final of threats.

Islands in the Sky is positive in attitude, as befits an adventure novel for adolescents. It presents the growth of a boy as a parallel for the growth of the race. And it says, as does Roy's uncle in the first line of the book, the best thing to do is not to worry, to "relax and enjoy yourself."

Such relaxation and enjoyment are only possible for Roy because he has thoroughly studied his aero- and astro-nautics, and only possible for the human race because it has learned so well how to protect itself with machines, to control at least part of its fall through space. In the last chapter of the novel,

"The Long Fall Home," Roy looks out the window of the ship that is taking him back to the surface of the planet, and sees, "with a shock that nearly jolted me out of my seat," that there is an "ominous red glow" coming from the ship's wing. A moment's thought assures him that everything is "really quite in order," that the glow is just the heat of their re-entry, but in that moment the structure of the novel is repeated. The book says again, as the serial structure says again and again, that, yes, the universe is dangerous, but, also yes, humans have learned to protect themselves from such dangers. The thing for a growing member of a growing race to do is to relax and enjoy the view. (The thing not to do, as *Against the Fall of Night* makes clear, is to huddle in fear inside a machine-run city, to refuse to look outward.)

The Sands of Mars is about the colonization of that planet. The novel follows the thoughts of one Martin Gibson, an author of best sellers, including science fiction, as he is a passenger on the maiden voyage of the first space liner to Mars, and as he observes the efforts the human race has made to settle itself on the red planet. In his personal growth, Gibson becomes a statement of the novel's argument that the human race must either "explore and master the material universe" or "simply stagnate on its own world." The book brings up the subject of an awed contemplation of the beauties of the universe, but it is really a celebration of humanity's powers to change the environment and to cause the desert to bloom.

As Gibson is flying up to the space station where he will catch the Martian liner, he looks down on the surface of the Earth and reflects that it is "chastening to think that all the thousands of years of human civilization had produced no appreciable change in the panorama below." (As Clarke points out in his Introduction to the 1967 reprint of the novel, Carl Sagan and others have used meteorological satellite photographs to prove that life cannot be detected even on our densely populated planet by orbiting satellites.) When Gibson is passing the Moon on the Martian liner, however, he sees on the surface of that body "minute sparks of light." The sparks were not there "fifty years ago"; they are "the lights of the first lunar cities, telling the stars that life [has] come at last to the Moon."

The suggestion that our companion world has been waiting, poetic overstatement as it may be, is also a claim of inevitability. The expansion of humanity to nearby worlds is seen as being as natural as growth or evolution. "We are at war, Mr. Gibson," says Hadfield, Mars' chief executive; "we're at war with Mars and all the forces it can bring against us—cold, lack of water, lack of air." And what the novel extols is humanity's ability to make for itself a new environment, to control—as it does in the spaceship itself—"the forces that [power] the stars themselves." At the end of the novel, the Martian colonists have developed a plant that will free the oxygen stored in the surface of the planet, and they have ignited one of their moons into a new sun. They have made for themselves a planet-size bubble of air, heat, and light like the space stations in *Islands in the Sky.*

The novel calls, as does *The Time Machine*, for a new way of seeing. Gibson is regularly warned that he "mustn't always believe" his eyes, and on board the space station he is able, looking out of the observation gallery at the heavens which seem to be whirling around him, to understand both how ancient men could have refused to believe that the solid Earth was rotating, and how his own "familiar divisions of day and night, of months and seasons, had no meaning here." The novel argues—contra Wells—that such a change in perspective can reveal, not that humanity is powerless before the great rhythms of Nature, but that the species can learn to make its own sunrise, one that—symbolically enough—rises out of the west rather than the east. The novel puts against the moment when Gibson, looking back from the liner, finally loses Earth, finally sees it disappear against the background of the Sun as though all its millions had been immolated, the fact that he is on the ship, that he is one representative of the human ability to escape being tied to a single planet.

The novel does summon up the awesome beauty of space. One of the officers on the Martian liner is Fred Hilton—"*the* Hilton" to Gibson—one of the three men to have survived the incredibly long journey to Saturn, to have stood on that planet's innermost moon and seen the giant world filling the sky. Gibson says to himself that there are "a good many things" he wants to talk to Hilton about before their trip is over.

But when the book comes to present Hilton's experience, to recapture the awe of what was seen on humanity's furthest voyage so far, Clarke falls back on simple description, on the sight of Saturn as seen from its moons. He clearly has Chesley Bonestell's well-known paintings in mind, and they are different enough from the sight of our Moon as seen from Earth to call up the awe produced by strangeness as well as by size. But that image alone is not enough to counterbalance the novel's concentration on humanity's successes in space. Martin Gibson does reflect, when he is outside the ship in a spacesuit, that "all men's voyagings and adventures" are "pitiful" when seen against the background of Andromeda, of the great nebula which he can cover with his thumbnail but which is as large a galaxy as the "sky-spanning ring" of the Milky Way. But the novel focuses instead—probably as a way of coping with the sheer immensity of the cosmos—on the world inside the ship and then on the great strides made by humans in the colonization of Mars.

Clarke may well have borrowed—in order to introduce the idea that humans will be improved by learning to sail across the abyss—from James Hilton's *Lost Horizon*. Clarke's Fred Hilton is very like James Hilton's Conway. Like Conway, Fred Hilton is reserved, does not become involved in trivia, and is something of a natural leader. Conway is the soul of equanimity, and Fred Hilton seems "to possess unlimited reserves of patience." The clearest parallel is when Clarke's Hilton is able—as is Conway in similar circumstances—to go to sleep in a dangerous situation simply because there is nothing more to be done about it until morning.

James Hilton's Conway is thoroughly self-possessed even before he is taken to Shangri-La, but Clarke's Hilton seems to have become calm and complete as a result of his visit to the Ultima Thule of the solar system. The nutshells and mosquito wings of existence (as Thoreau would call them) do not bother Clarke's Hilton because he has looked upon the ultimate; he has been to "the cold outer giants of the Sun's scattered family," and he has "returned again to the light and warmth of the inner worlds." And like Conway, he will go again if he can, even if this time he will be one of those who does not return.

As I have said, the novel's focus is elsewhere. In space Martin Gibson does have awesome revelations; he does, for example, suddenly realize that the stars are "all around him, down to the horizon he no longer [possesses], and even below, under his feet." But the novel as a whole directs attention away from this lost horizon; it focuses on humanity's achievements in space. When the ship first picks up Mars' radio beacon, Gibson can hear only "the hiss and crackle of radio noise," "the voices of the stars and nebulae," "radiations that had set out upon their journey before the birth of Man." But when he hears "the infinitely faint undulating whistle that [is] breaking through the cosmic storm," he knows it is the sign of human presence.

Gibson also knows that there may be, that "there must be," although "lost beyond recall," "buried far down in the depths of the crackling, whispering chaos . . . the sounds of alien civilizations talking to one another." And the novel itself seems to cope with the awesome size of space, not only by concentrating on human accomplishments, but also by assuming that there must be other beings in the universe. When Gibson tours the Martian liner, which is itself round like a world, he receives "one of his strongest impressions" from "the empty passenger quarters." "A house so new that no one has ever lived in it," he reflects, "can be more lonely than an old, deserted ruin that has once known life and may still be peopled by ghosts." The novel escapes having the old ruin of Mars be lonely by having it be inhabited by a friendly, cowlike life, one very different from Wells' "tenacled monstrosities" or Edgar Rice Burroughs' Martian princesses, but life still. We are not alone in this gigantic cosmos.

But as I keep repeating, the novel's primary means of dealing with the awesomeness of space remains the redirection of attention, the focus on human accomplishments. When Martin Gibson looks back on Earth from the observation lounge of the Martian liner, he thinks: "Well, this is it. . . . Down there is all my past life, and the lives of all my ancestors back to the first blob of jelly in the first primal sea. . . . Down beneath those clouds lies the whole of human history; soon I shall be able to eclipse with my little finger what was, until a lifetime ago, all of Man's dominion and everything that his art had saved from time." The use of the phrase "a lifetime ago" makes explicit the novel's assumption that if the individual can look down on Earth and identify with all of the previous lives back to the first blob, then he certainly ought to be able to identify in imagination with all of the race's future lives, and thus with the future accomplishments of the race. In fact, to make concrete this potential identification, the novel has Gibson recognize in the youngest member of the ship's crew the son he did not even know he had.

When Gibson was at Cambridge, he fell in love with another student. The affair was hard on his academic work, however, a fact he blamed on the young woman, and after he had to leave college he suffered a breakdown. Since then, he has not allowed himself any close human involvements, and the novel uses his growing realization of his connection with the past and the future, with the woman he left and the son he now acknowledges, to present its thesis that the way to live in a universe in which we must die is to identify with the life of the race. The death that ends individuals takes longer to end species, and it just may be that this one species may grow to control a larger share of the universe than now seems possible.

The willingness to give the future to our children, not to resent the fact that they will be alive when we are dead, the willingness to make for them a start on a future worth having, is a way of looking away from our own graves and from the awesome size of the universe. Martin Gibson (give son?) not only acknowledges his child, but also finds that there is on Mars a work he can identify with, can give his life to. He has, since college, lived for himself alone. In boarding the Martian liner he has, "for the first time in almost as long as he [can] remember . . . given his future entirely into the keeping of others." This trust, this willingness to join, grows on Mars into "a longing to identify himself with their [the colonists'] work, wherever it might lead." At a community sing, a form of entertainment he usually avoids, Gibson finds himself entering in, realizing that he is surrounded by "men and women united in a single task, driving towards a common goal, each knowing that their work was vital to the community." He has always been "an outsider," but now he wants "to join in the game." He has, as a novelist, "never had the slightest use for those many Victorian parables about lazy, self-centered men becoming useful members of the community," but he has "a horrible fear that something uncommonly like this was beginning to happen to him."

Gibson's personal growth has even wider implications. As the novel makes clear at the end, he will in time take over the job of Chief Executive. The imagination he has used to write novels about the future of the human race on other worlds will turn out to be exactly the quality that fits him for leadership of the Martian colony. The conversation he has in the first chapter with the pilot who is to fly him up to the space station hints at this very point. If the pilot is able, because he really does what Gibson has only written of doing, to be a little condescending, he is also more than a little prosaic. He will never make himself spacesick, as Gibson does (just by imagining spacesickness), but at the same time he will never have the ability, as Gibson does, to imagine an achievable future, a Mars as it might be.

In fact, as Gibson's stories have become better, as he "has cut out the blood and thunder" and gotten "interested in fundamentals," as he has learned to "hang on to something solid" (as the pilot advises him to do in free fall), so he has learned to use his imagination as does Hadfield, the current Chief Executive: to dream of a future that might really come to pass. (Hadfield's name—he has the field but his day will pass—and the fact that he is just as often called by his job title make it clear that the position is more important than the individual, and that Gibson's stepping into the role is part of the novel's thesis that the race is more important than the individual.)

The book ends, then, not just with the major event, the manufactured sunrise of "Project Dawn," but with the projected future growth of Gibson, with his discovery of surprising powers within himself and with the continuing suggestion that—as Gibson is representative of the race itself—humanity will find similar surprising powers within itself. As both the Martian liner and the newly ignited sun build upon the forces loosed by "dying atoms," so the future builds upon the dead past and the dying present.

Prelude to Space was published the year before *Islands in the Sky* and *The Sands of Mars*, but—because it has much in common with Clarke's nonfiction explanations and justifications of space flight (one of which, *The Exploration of Space*, was a Book-of-the-Month Club selection in 1952)—it offers a more straightforward summary than do the other two novels of what we have seen about the fiction Clarke wrote before, during, and just after World War II.

The central character, Dirk Alexson, a University of Chicago historian on leave to cover the first trip to the Moon, begins with something of a bias against science. He has something of that "fear of science" which has "been common since the great discoveries of the Victorian era." He wonders whether scientists are not "a lot of Frankensteins," "merely interested in a technical project without any regard for its consequences."

By the mid-point of the book, Alexson has realized that his fear of science is—or was (he recovers from it)—a part of humanity's larger fear of the unknown, its fear of all that can be represented by the dark of outer space. He had wondered whether humanity was "ready to be pitchforked out into space, ready to face the challenge of barren and inhospitable worlds never meant for Man." He was, "subconsciously," afraid that space flight "was too big a thing for Man"; "like Pascal," he "was terrified by the silence and the emptiness of infinite space."

The idea that there may be in the universe "worlds never meant for Man" is represented in the novel—intelligently, but briefly—by C. S. Lewis, who is quoted as saying that the unimaginable distances of outer space are "God's quarantine regulations." The same idea is represented—stupidly—by a religious fanatic who tries to sabotage the *Prometheus*, the ship that is to carry the first humans to the Moon. The religious fanatic, symbolically enough, manages to kill himself out of fear; he does not realize that the "metal claws" of a robot are trying to save him; he dies as a result of exposing himself to radioactive materials whose nature he does not understand. He dies as Clarke fears the race will die if it does not explore the material universe: out of ignorance.

Alexson learns that the scientists he is observing are not like "the coldly passionless scientist of fiction" (instead, they are "fully aware of the implications of [their] work"); he also learns that they are children, in the Wordsworthian sense. They have not lost the child's sense of wonder at the universe; they are like "Newton's description of himself as a small child picking up brightly colored pebbles on the shore of the ocean of knowledge." Their leader is even named Sir Robert Derwent, and he is no more "ashamed of wanting to play with spaceships" than was Wordsworth of having grown up within the sound of Derwent Water. And Clarke's Derwent is perfectly willing to agree that his play will certainly "change the world"; that it may "perhaps" even change "the universe."

"The first men seriously to advance the idea of interplanetary travel were visionaries in love with a dream," says Alexson. "The fact that they were also technicians doesn't matter—they were, essentially, artists using their science to create something new." The space program continues to be run, he concludes, by similar "visionaries, poets if you will, who also happen to be scientists." They would cross space "for no other reason than to watch the Earth turning from night to day above the glittering lunar peaks, or to see Saturn's rings, in all their unimaginable glory, bridging the sky of his nearest moon."

Two nights before the launch, however, when Sir Robert is trying to relax by flipping through a volume of Swinburne he read as a boy, the poetry he still finds himself able to respond to is full more of fear than of wonder. He can no longer hear "Love's lute" as sufficient music in "the lands of Death." He no longer cares that by "the tideless dolorous midland sea," in the "land of sand and ruin and gold," there "shone one woman and none but she." He does still care that there will be a time when neither

> star nor sun shall waken,
>   Nor any change of light:
> Nor sound of waters shaken,

> Nor any sound or sight:
> Nor wintry leaves nor vernal,
> Nor days nor things diurnal;
> Only the sleep eternal
> In an eternal night.

The "eternal night" will come, he agrees, "and too soon for Man's liking." "But at least before they guttered and died, [Man] would have known the stars; before it faded like a dream, the Universe would have yielded up its secrets to his mind. Or if not to his, then to the minds that would come after and would finish what he had now begun." Sir Robert's vision goes beyond just seeing Earth from the Moon, or Saturn from its nearest moon; he wants to be part of the attempt to understand the universe.

The confrontation between the fear of the final dark and the hope of understanding represented by space travel takes place most openly at, appropriately enough, Hyde Park Corner. There, one speaker is "engaged in proving, apparently with the aid of Biblical texts, that Doomsday [is] at hand." Another speaker, "an elderly, white-haired man," argues that the universe is "not hostile to life, but merely indifferent"; that its indifference is both "an opportunity and a challenge"—a challenge to make come true the words G. B. Shaw put into the mouth of Lilith in *Back to Methuselah*: "Of life only there is no end; and though of its million starry mansions many are empty and many still unbuilt, and though its vast domain is as yet unbearably desert, my seed shall one day fill it and master it to its uttermost confines."

Eric Rabkin has suggested that this elderly, white-haired gentleman is meant to be a "homage to Stapledon." The elderly man's thesis is more positive than that, however; Stapledon sees the human drama as finally tragic, but this speaker sees it as finally epic, as a triumphant conquering of the material universe.

Be that as it may, the novel puts against the vision of

Doomsday (religion's or science's) the hope that space travel is the next step on the way to understanding the universe. And on the way to saying that, it touches on topics Clarke explored in all his early fiction. It sees space travel as an escape from social stagnation, as a way of giving a purpose to humanity, and as a way of extending the life of the species.

The attractiveness of racial stagnation, of decadence, is represented in the novel—rather daringly—by London itself. The city is presented as being in part unchanging. The "New" bridge is forty years old, the skyline is still dominated by St. Paul's, and South Kensington is as full of science students as it was in H. G. Wells' day. "Sunday morning rides" will "still be cantering their fine horses" along "the wide sands of Rotten Row," thinks one of the astronauts, and not with disapproval, "when humanity's first ships [are] turning homeward from the stars."

At the same time, as Alexson notices, "buildings older than the United States" bear signs such as "Grosvenor Radio and Electronic Corporation." The city is changing, as it must:

> Civilization could never stand still. Over the very ground on which he was walking [the Embankment], the mammoths had once come trampling through the rushes at the river's edge. They, and not the ape-men watching from their caves, had been the masters of this land. But the day of the ape had dawned at last; the forests and swamps had given way before the might of his machines. Dirk knew now that the story was merely beginning. Even at this moment, on far worlds beneath strange suns, Time and the Gods were preparing for Man the sites of cities yet to be.

As in *Islands in the Sky* and *The Sands of Mars*, the protagonist's discovery of a sense of purpose in his own life is a repetition of the book's theme that space flight will give the race a purpose. Alexson had been looking for a work he could give his life to, and in chronicling the first trip to the Moon he finds that purpose larger than himself which is a solace in this world where the individual must die. As Alexson is leaving one part of the project for the last time, he realizes "with a pang" that he is also "saying good-bye to one of the happiest periods of his life. It had been happy because it had been full, because it had extended all his resources to the utmost—above all, because he had been among men whose lives had a purpose which they knew was greater than themselves."

But the basic reason for space travel remains continued life and knowledge for the race. At the end of the novel, in an Epilogue set on New Year's Eve, 1999, twenty years after the successful completion of the *Prometheus'* first flight, we find Dirk Alexson living on the Moon. He has "parted from waves and clouds, from winds and rainbows, from blue skies and the long twilights of summer evenings," we find out, in order to receive "an indefinite stay of execution." He has a weak heart which, on Earth, would have quit long ago, but which under the weak gravity of the Moon may well give him a life longer than that usually allotted to humans.

Similarly, we are reminded that the race as a whole was threatened by ice ages in the past. "No doubt in prehistoric times there were those who shook their heads and prophesied disaster when the young men of the tribe went in search of new lands in the terrifying, unknown world around them. Yet it was well that the search had been made before the glaciers came grinding down from the Pole."

The glaciers will "return" one day, of that we may be sure. But that is "the least of the dooms" that may "descend upon the Earth." "There comes a time in the life of every star when the delicate balance of its atomic furnace must tilt, one way or the other. In the far future the descendants of Man [may] catch, from the safety of the outermost planets, a last glimpse of their birthplace as it [sinks] into the fires of the detonating Sun."

More immediately, we are warned that "atomic power

makes interplanetary travel not only possible but imperative."
On Earth humanity has "too many eggs in one rather fragile
basket." Space flight will allow "energies that might have gone
to make wars" to "be fully employed in the colonization of the
planets." As Alexson is listening to the countdown for the
Prometheus' first flight, he is reminded of another morning
thirty years before, "when another group of scientists . . .
stood watching in another desert, preparing to unleash the
energies that power the suns." The decision is humanity's; the
race can destroy itself in its own atomic furnace or use the
knowledge to continue to exist and to grow. It can resolve, as
the director of the space project suggests, to "take no frontiers
into space."

Even short of destruction, the alternative to space flight is
to remain, as do the aborigines watching the takeoff of the
Prometheus from the hills surrounding its Australian launch
site, too content and well adjusted to the environment, its
slave and not its master.

Interestingly enough, when Clarke comes to describe the
importance of the *Prometheus*' flight, he reverses his use of
primitive peoples. Space flight is a way of escaping "the tribal
conflicts of the early twentieth century," but it also is compared to the first canoe leaving a South Sea island for the
other islands on the horizon; the *Prometheus* becomes the first
canoe to sail "beyond the lagoon, past the friendly shelter of
the coral reef . . . into the unknown perils and wonders of the
open sea." The change allows, of course, room for growth; we
can extrapolate a future civilization as far beyond ours as ours
is beyond that first canoe.

The book ends, not just with Dirk Alexson on the Moon
waiting for a new year, a new century, and a new millennium,
but with the hope that the race will become, if not a god, at
least godlike. The savages in Borneo, it is suggested, may
make one of *Prometheus*' rocket stages a "tribal god"; but the
novel would hope that the human tribe will become as godlike

as the idea of taking fire back to the heavens suggests. The novel is, as Alexson as much as says, a statement on the positive side in "the ancient conflict between pessimism and optimism, between those who [believe] in Man and those who [do] not."

5

Childhood's End

CLARKE was no more free of the awakening into nightmare that was the 1950s than was anyone else. Like the rest of us, he came out of the euphoria at the end of World War II gradually. He became aware—as did we all—that the insane was more than just possible, that the two superpowers could and might put an end to the race. The discovery touches *Islands in the Sky*, in that moment when the boys seem threatened by the canister of radioactive waste; but it *governs* the fiction Clarke wrote in the fifties, especially his (in my opinion) most important book, *Childhood's End* (1953). That novel becomes a magnificently desperate attempt to continue to hope for a future for the race in the face of mounting evidence to the contrary. It becomes, in fact, a sometimes brilliant attempt to turn the contrary evidence to the positive. It becomes nothing less than an effort to make positive the destruction of the race.

Earthlight, a short novel first published in 1951 (expanded in 1955), offers a good introduction to *Childhood's End* because it tries to be positive, as the three novels treated in the previous chapter are positive, by hoping that the human race will escape its internal conflicts by escaping into space. *Earthlight* ends, as does *Prelude to Space*, with the hope that there will be no more wars, that "the inexhaustible wealth" of the other planets will keep the race from ever again being "divided against itself." Cheerful as such a hope is, the book is in some ways (and I think basically) divided against itself.

Earthlight has several things in common with *Islands in the Sky*, *The Sands of Mars*, and *Prelude to Space*. It gives a picture of humanity's success in the war against Nature, a war being waged in this case on the Moon, Mars, Venus, and the satellites of the outer planets. It pictures scientific discoveries as being usable in two ways, to perfect as well as to destroy human life. And it features a protagonist who has to widen his sympathies, who has to learn to appreciate those who have settled on the other planets as well as those who have chosen to remain on Earth. More basically, the protagonist also learns to have enough faith in the future of the human race to decide to sire a child.

It is this last which can act as an indication of the divided nature of the novel. There is no scene in which the protagonist actually decides to put aside his previous hesitations and become a parent. At the end of the book we know he has done so, but his moment of most serious doubt comes after he has written to his wife that he has overcome his doubts. There is no corresponding scene of reaffirmation. It seems that we are to assume that the general hopefulness about the future of humanity which follows upon the novel's chief incident, the brief battle between Earth and its colonies on the other planets, is to extend to the protagonist too. But the hopefulness does not, in fact, sweep the whole book before it. It is, as is the decision to have a child, testified to; but, as we shall see, in important ways the novel itself remains unconvinced.

Earthlight wants to believe that the human race will not destroy itself, and it wants to say so by juxtaposing a scene in which humans are at war with a scene in which humans rescue their former enemies. It is a version of the destroyer sinking the submarine and then standing by to pick up survivors. The battle, we are told, is seen by both sides as so pointless—and is in fact so destructive—that both governments are thrown out and humanity's better instincts prevail. The protagonist, who was a counterspy for Earth, and his former antagonist, who was a spy for the other planets, have a drink together in the novel's last scene because they can both acknowledge now that they were caught up in a movement larger than themselves, that their differences were just different reactions to the inevitability of humanity's leaving its home planet. That is why, in the story, the protagonist does not manage to catch the antagonist; the historical movement is too large for individuals to do much about. But, at the same time, the novel does not have a closing scene to match its opening chapter; it does not have a positive sunrise to match the coming of lunar night with which it begins. The rescue scene is more interested in the fact that people probably can survive for a few minutes in the vacuum of space than it is in countering the centrality of the battle scene. The scene in which two other characters manage to escape from the dry quicksand on the Moon does not become—as it clearly was meant to be—a convincing example of humanity escaping from the trap of its past, of its use of war to solve disagreements.

The problem is that the battle scene itself is beautiful. It is—as are most such scenes in science fiction and in science-fiction films—as attractive as a fireworks display (war and disaster films, for that matter, have the same difficulty). We are unable to forget—in the midst of rescue missions and drinks with former enemies—the flashing lights and silently bursting fireballs of the novel's battle on the Moon. The war is in Technicolor; the peace in black and white.

In fact, Clarke begs the question somewhat by having this last battle of humanity's last war take place after the race has managed to leave its home planet. As the novel points out, total war between the planets and Earth is impossible. Given such distances, it is pointless to imagine space fleets and the invasion of whole planets. The only war possible is that which takes place in the book, the "duel" between the conservative fortress and the innovative spaceships, between those who would keep humanity at home and those who would explore the universe. The real threat of superweapons—at least as it was experienced in the 1950s—does not come up. There is no consideration of the possible destruction of the planet on which humanity is so far confined. Clarke bypasses that possibility in favor of a future battle that does not menace the whole race.

The atomic threat is still there, however, underlying the novel. Even though the race seems to have escaped our planet without a disastrous final war, even though the novel ends with a toast in hope of no more wars, the beautiful battle scene remains at the center of the story, not quite matched by any other incident. The book itself admits that there is a "deadly glamor" to war, and it reflects more than once that the structures humans have built in their war with Nature will not be able to withstand the attacks of humans. "The dark domes," thinks the protagonist, as he looks at a Moon settlement, give "so little sign of the life and light" they hold. "They had been built to withstand the forces that Nature could bring against them—but how pitiably fragile they would be if ever they faced the fury of Man."

The main action of the novel is seen against a background of a supernova that suddenly appears in the constellation Draco (the Dragon). Novas, we are told by one of the characters, happen about a hundred times a year in our galaxy, and since one in ten suns probably has planets, it would seem, as the protagonist realizes, that "at any moment, as likely as not, *somewhere* in the universe a whole solar system, with strangely peopled worlds and civilizations, [is] being tossed carelessly into a cosmic furnace." Life is "a fragile and delicate phenomenon," he concludes, "poised on the razor's edge between cold and heat."

But the protagonist does not stop there. Thinking of the threat of war, he goes on to say that Man does not seem "content with the hazards that Nature [can] provide. He [seems to be] busily building his own funeral pyre."

That thought, it seems to me, is too much for this novel. It does not apply to the only kind of war possible to a race scattered over several planets; it applies to a race trapped on a single planet. It is a thought out of the 1950s that insists on being said, even though the novel is set two hundred years in the future. It addresses the threat of racial annihilation in a future when such annihilation is—by the book's own statement—impossible.

Earthlight wants to say that *Nova Draconis* is not a sign. It wants to believe that although the heavens may "blaze with portents," the galaxy "burn with the beacon lights of detonating stars," Man will "go about his own affairs with sublime indifference." He will "not be overawed" by anything the stars can do; "in his own good time," he will "deal with them" as he sees fit. But the novel also fears that, although the nova has "crowded politics off the front page," it will not be for long. Humanity, the book says, cannot "bear to think of eternity for long." The nova "turned men's minds for a moment from their own affairs and made them think of ultimate realities," but after that moment "the fierce violet light of the greatest nova in history shone now on a divided system, upon planets that had ceased to threaten each other and were now preparing for deeds." The novel seems to feel, in the "catalogue of disagreements and countercharges, of threats barely veiled by the euphemisms of diplomacy . . . the inhuman cold of the lunar night seeping through the walls." It fears that the uncaring nature of the universe and the belligerent nature of the human race may prove to be too much alike to keep us from destruction.

Thomas D. Clareson has objected to the use of the nova in *Earthlight* because, although it does permit "reflections upon the fragility of life . . . it does not attain a unifying symbolic value." It does not, and I think that failure is itself a sign that the novel is afraid the nova may become a portent. The book is unable to escape the decade in which it was written; it is afraid of the very catastrophe it would like to assume we will escape.

The novel wants to hope that humans will one day control more of the universe, as they now control the world under the domes of the Moon's cities. (There they can make both thunderstorms and rainbows at will.) The book wants to hope that humans may be able to do in a larger sense what they can already do on the slow-turning Moon, to travel quickly enough to "hold the sun on the horizon," to someday control even time. But the book fears that the scene of lunar night with which it opens may be more prophetic; it fears that humanity may pass as does a flash of light in the dark. When the protagonist is racing across the Moon in the novel's opening chapter, a scene not matched by anything at the end of the book, he is aware of coming out of the lunar night into a few minutes of sunshine, of seeing the monorail on which he is riding "as an unsupported ribbon of light, a filament of flame built by sorcery rather than by human engineering." But when the rail dips back down into a valley, and darkness veils "the gossamer bridges and the canyon-fringing curves," only the mountain peaks seem "still magically afloat upon the sea of night that [laps] around them." And in a little while even "those proud peaks" surrender "to the night." The novel fears that just as it plays itself out against the background of long time and slow change represented by the surface of the Moon, so the race itself may one day be represented by the monument to the dead in the Sea of Rains, by the rust-free wrecks and undisturbed vehicle tracks which will remain until the Moon itself passes away.

The book would like to believe that the human race will

spread itself out from its home planet as does the light from a
nova, but it fears that we may pass away as do our radio
waves, finally "obliterated by the ceaseless radio whispering of
the stars." It would like to believe that the antagonist's suggestion that humanity be allowed to destroy itself ("Fire is a good
sterilizer") is an overstatement, but it fears that the same man
is wise when he takes comfort in all of the life forms in all of
the systems which must be seeing the nova; at least from that
perspective our own failure—if we fail—is not seen as life's
only chance.

Clarke says of his protagonist that he always tries "to take
the long view," especially when he is "depressed by the current
situation." *Earthlight* itself, it seems to me, is a similar attempt; and as such it testifies to the terrifying nature of the
decade in which it was written.

The end of childhood, its fulfillment as well as its termina-
tion, is, at the conclusion of Clarke's novel *Childhood's End*,
the evolution of humanity into a galaxy-wide and still-growing
Overmind. The invaders from outer space, the Overlords, it
turns out, have come to Earth because humanity is one of the
aristocrats of the universe after all. Like princes raised in the
forest by peasants, our children will grow up to inherit the
starry kingdom we always more than half assumed they
would inherit.

The nature of their inheritance, however, especially the loss
of individuality in the Overmind, reminds us that princes almost always find that being king is something other than they
expected. We have long thought it likely that our children
would one day visit the stars, using ships for that matter very
like those of the Overlords; but by the end of the novel it is
clear that, although the descendants of humanity have inherited the heavens, such is not exactly what we meant.

In the more profound sense the novel is about becoming
adult, about realizing not only that most human hopes are

frustrated, but that even those hopes which are fulfilled are fulfilled in ways not expected, often in ways not imaginable. The end of childhood is adulthood, and in *Childhood's End* adulthood is defined as having come to appreciate that, for the race as for the individual, while hindsight may suggest that the present was implicit in the past, it does not follow that the future—and whatever revelations it may have about the importance of intelligent life in the universe—can be anticipated from the present.

By way of overture to such a theme, the novel opens with a comparison of two ex-German rocket scientists, one of whom chose the East and the other the West. In spite of this reference to the arms race, the contrast is less between political systems than between two human attitudes: Konrad Schneider's somewhat childish hope of being the first human to launch a rocket into space, and Reinhold Hoffman's more adult hope of helping the human race to take the first step to whatever secrets the stars may hold.

For Schneider, the result of the arrival of the Overlords' ship is despair; but for Hoffman, whom we see against a background of star-filled sky, the result is the comforting assurance that we are not alone, that the stars are neither so "aloof" nor so "indifferent" as they have always seemed. Hoffman can feel no regret, not even for the loss of a lifetime's work, because the giant ships have answered his most profound question more fully than any rocket to the Moon could have.

It is exactly this need of Hoffman's, his hunger for other beings with which to share the contemplation of this universe, which is finally answered for the race by the Overmind, though long after Hoffman's death and in a way he could no more have dreamt of than he dreamt that the stars would come to him. From the vantage point of the conclusion of the novel we can look back and see the existence of the Overmind as somewhat implicit in the human urge to reach for the stars, but from the timebound vantage point of Reinhold Hoffman we can see only the positive reply to our hope that we are not alone, that the existence of intelligent life is not a one-time accident.

The first story the novel has to tell is of how former U.N. Secretary-General Rikki Stormgren is able to be content with the relationship between the Overlords and humans only after he has attained the unchildish age of ninety. He takes so long, not because he fails to appreciate how much the rule of the Overlords has improved the lot of humanity, or because he agrees with the ex-preacher who says that freedom is lost when a God whose will is unclear is replaced by a godlike being whose will is perfectly clear, but because, when he is still in the relative childishness of his sixties, he shares with both the ex-preacher and the blind leader of the anti-Overlord under-ground the obsession with seeing what the chief Overlord, Karellen, looks like. As far as Stormgren is concerned, the only freedoms humans have sacrificed to live under the rule of the Overlords are the freedoms to make war or to cause people to starve. Such a loss, of course, is hardly enough to make him fear that false gods are being put before the true. But the abrupt flash of a meteor overhead—while he stands one night in his penthouse garden—reminds him that life is short, that, while in a hundred years Karellen will still be leading mankind toward the goal only the Overlord can see, little time is left if he hopes to discover what is behind the "darkened screen" in the Overlord's ship.

What Stormgren wants to see, of course, is not only what Karellen looks like, but also the Overlord's ultimate goal. Without quite realizing it, he hopes to infer the one from the other. It is one of the beauties of the book that what he finally sees behind the screen is only what Karellen has prepared him to see. Even though the Secretary-General knows that the Overlord's "very slips of the tongue are calculated to several decimal places," he is still misled by various references to "failures" and to humanity's "long memory" to assume that he recognizes the devil-form behind the screen because the Overlords have visited Earth before. What he concludes—and becomes content with—is what he in fact already knows from his years of service to Karellen, that the seeming devils are really guardian angels, that humanity is, has been, and will be cared for.

In the sense that what he learns is what he already knows, Stormgren could have learned almost as much from the flash of the meteor. As its trail glows for a while and then dies, so it is a sign of the brevity of life. As it is described as a "shining spear" thrust through "the dome of the sky," so it is a sign of how childish is our illusion that the sky is a roof. And as the stars seem more noticeable after its fading, so it is a sign that —as Reinhold Hoffman knows—if humanity has a future, it must have something to do with those stars overhead, those lights in the sky which have outlasted so many fadings. The interpretation of what we see, in other words, is—as we all know—bound by what we allow ourselves to see.

When Karellen does finally show himself to the race as a whole, standing in the door of his ship with two human children in his arms, the tableau thus created is open to three interpretations. The first, leapt to by most people as it was by Stormgren, is that the two races have met before. The second interpretation, which is truer, is that the Overlords have come to take care of the children of humanity. The third, which turns out to be the truest, and which is hinted at when the parents of the two children remember the story of the Pied Piper, is that the Overlords have come to carry off the children of humanity. As we read the novel, we come to the adult awareness that each generation can only be wise unto its limits, that the discovery of truth is an evolutionary process.

The major revelation of the second section of the novel, which is that "the stars are not for Man," also comes in stages. At first it seems as if the Overlords have come between the human race and outer space because we were threatening to carry our wars to the other planets. Another rooftop scene, matching that of Stormgren in his penthouse garden, makes it clear that—as Karellen later says—humans cannot face the "stupendous challenge" of deep space.

The rooftop scene takes place during the cocktail party which is the central action of this, the utopian, section of the novel. Two men, George Greggson and Jan Rodricks, each momentarily frustrated in love and thus out of patience with the party and the world it symbolizes, retire separately to the rooftop garden of their host's fine African house.

Greggson's first impression as he looks out over a great basin, swampland, and jungle is that he is monarch of all he surveys. As his eye focuses on a great wall of mountains to the west, and on the sunset behind them, he is awed into sobriety by the sizes and distances in front of him. As the stars rush out with tropical suddenness, he realizes that, Alaskan that he is, he cannot find any familiar constellations, not even the Southern Cross. Feeling lost and dazzled by size, he decides to return to the party and to the warmth of other people.

Jan Rodricks, on the other hand, as did Stormgren on a similar night, sees a meteor in the sky. He also sees the meteoric trail of an Overlord ship headed out to the stars, and the combination of sights makes him wish he could, as he eventually does, make the same voyage.

When Rodricks returns from that voyage, however, he returns aware that he has not been able to comprehend much of what he has seen. He also returns dreadfully homesick, even for a planet which has aged eighty years since he left. His reaction to the size of the universe, in other words, is finally the same as Greggson's. Both men would have to agree with Karellen when he displayed some pictures taken in deep space and says: "Your race, in its present stage of evolution, cannot face that stupendous challenge . . . the stars are not for Man."

Even were Karellen not to say so, the means of Rodricks' voyage would suggest that the stars are not for Man. Rodricks stows away in the belly of a stuffed whale, part of a life-size mock-up the Overlords are sending back to their home planet. The episode, properly understood, argues that Rodricks needs as much protection in outer space as Jonah needed to survive in that other alien environment, the sea.

Rodricks himself takes an undersea voyage which explains the point of the model of the whale (which is presented as being locked in a struggle with a giant squid). What the would-be space traveler finds in the ocean is a part of his own planet that is as "unknown as anything he might meet beyond the stars," "a realm of nightmare creatures preying on each other in a darkness undisturbed since the world began." It is a realm not badly represented by the battle between the whale and the squid, a world in which an unprotected human would be instantly dead.

Rodricks visits the underwater research station of a Professor Sullivan, and there he finds, as did Roy Malcolm in *Islands in the Sky*, that a giant bubble of air and light is absolutely necessary to human survival in such an alien environment. Although Professor Sullivan has learned to control some undersea dangers—the giant squid, Lucifer, for example, which has been turned into a pet—still he knows that as "Lucey" is always dangerous so he has in the sea "an enemy" that never rests, that one day will take advantage of a mistake of his to crush him and his little kingdom. And knowing such, it is no wonder that Sullivan is given to an absent-minded fondling of fish skulls and to thinking a lot about death.

Karellen himself explains how we are to take Rodricks' stowing away inside the creature from Sullivan's realm. Studying the giant model, the Overlord reflects upon the story of Jonah, remarking as he does so that it is a story about a man protected in an alien environment. His emphasis is typical of the Overlords' protective attitude toward humanity, but it also makes clear why the story of Jonah is a better precedent than, say, that of the Trojan horse. While it is true that Rodricks wants to invade the citadel of the Overlords, the main point of his stowing away is to underline just how fragile human beings are. That Rodricks has to put himself into a state of suspended animation, that he needs the protection of the best science of both humanity and the Overlords, and that his family and friends cannot possibly live long enough to see him return all argue that the stars are not for Man.

The great revelation of the novel's last section at first seems to be that the stars are, if not for Man, at least for the children of Man. But that we always knew; we always assumed that the stars were not for us but for future generations. The great revelation of the novel's last section is that the children of Man will no longer be human.

When Jan Rodricks returns from space, he knows at last "how vain" had been "the dream that . . . lured him to the stars." Having "glimpsed the universe in all its awful immensity," he now knows it is "no place for Man." He also realizes, to our surprise as much as his, that the stars are not for the Overlords either, at least not in any very comprehensive sense.

Even though the minds of the Overlords are "ten—perhaps a hundred—times as powerful as men's," "in the final reckoning" it makes "no difference"; the Overlords are finally as "helpless" as humanity, are "equally overwhelmed by the unimaginable complexity of a galaxy of a hundred thousand million suns, and a cosmos of a hundred thousand million galaxies." Faced with such immensity, humans and Overlords alike become as impotent as the giant Cyclopean eye the Overlords have in their museum: they can but stare.

On the other hand, when George Greggson flees the loneliness of the rooftop garden to avoid thinking about exactly such topics, he runs into another experience as awesome in its implications as anything suggested to him by the nighttime sky. He finds himself at a new and improved Ouija board, one which reflects hundreds of starlike points of light from the ball bearings that make up its almost frictionless surface. He has to confront the something that spells out "BELIEVE IN MAN" and "NATURE IS WITH YOU." He has to realize, first in the premonitions of his wife and then later in the telepathic powers of their children, that there is an "I AM ALL" of which humanity is to become a part. He has to begin to reconcile himself to the fact that the race will give up its individual future to a greater whole which can come closer to understanding the cosmos. He has to resign himself to the discovery that the way to the stars turns out to be, not the atomic power of the physicist, but the metaphysicist's desire for the infinite.

The difference between humanity and the Overlords, then, is that while the latter are the more intelligent, the former have a more intense desire for the whole. It is a difference that is there in Hoffman's refusal to begrudge the loss of his life's work, in Stormgren's inability to care whether humans are losing their independence, and most especially at the Ouija board. While the Overlord Rashaverak can only sit aside and observe, the humans at the table are able to surrender themselves to the larger whole, to the group experience. It may be, as one of the Overlords asserts, that "mysticism" is "the prime aberration of the human mind," but if so, in a novel where mysticism seems to mean that no human wants to be an island, the Overlords—who are unable to evolve into the Overmind —might well envy such a universal abnormality.

On their own planet, the Overlords live in separate cities, each of which is dedicated to a particular specialty. On Earth, humans try to build a community, the New Athens, which will combine all specialties into a whole. The long-lived Overlords will continue to serve the Overmind, says Karellen, but in that service they will "not lose their souls." Short-lived humans, on the other hand, have always had to give up their souls in this sense; they have always had to surrender their individual hopes to the future of the race.

So, although Jan Rodricks looks like a child sitting there in the Overlords' giant chair at the end of the novel, he is in fact to be seen as more adult than they are. We are to see him as typical of all humans when he—the last man—wants to remain on the Earth the children of Man are about to destroy and absorb on the way to becoming part of the Overmind. We are to sympathize completely with his inability to care about any life he might be able to lead away from this planet where his kind lived and died.

Childhood's End is not the only story of Clarke's to argue that humanity has a tendency to want to become a whole, that such an evolution may be implicit in the race. "Rescue Party," Clarke's second published story, is—as I have said—largely about the human race's rescuing itself from the Sun's becoming a nova. But the description of that rescue is more than a little suggestive of a step toward the Overmind.

One of the nonhumans on the rescue ship from the Galactic Federation is a representative of "the strange beings from the system of Palador." The Paladorian is "a mobile but still dependent cell in the consciousness of its race." It is bound to the other individuals of its kind as "inexorably" as are "the living cells of the human body." This arrangement, the story says, is wonderfully powerful. "In moments of crisis, the single units comprising the Paladorian mind [can] link together in an organization no less close than that of any physical brain. At such moments they [form] an intellect more powerful than any other in the Universe." One of the other nonhumans, in fact, has written a book "trying to prove that eventually all intelligent races [will] sacrifice individual consciousness and that one day only group minds [will] remain in the Universe."

Be that as it may, the humans in "Rescue Party" are certainly described as working together. The nonhumans find on the deserted Earth that the race has managed to record and store "five thousand million punched cards holding all that could be recorded of each man, woman, and child on the planet"—surely a step in the unification of the species. So too they find "records of all the laws that Man had ever passed, and all the speeches that had ever been made in his council chambers." But the real suggestion that some large oneness may be the ultimate direction of the race can be seen in the description of the gigantic fleet of rockets that humans have used to evacuate their planet. "Lying across league after league of space, ranged in a vast three-dimensional array of rows and columns with the precision of a marching army, were thousands of tiny pencils of light. They were moving swiftly; the whole immense lattice holding its shape as a single unit." Such a description adds meaning to the first officer's speech I quoted in chapter 4: "The whole race must have embarked on this journey in the hope that its descendants would complete it, generations later." One of the many possible futures which seem potentially there in the human race as we know it is the eventual loss of individual consciousness and the formation of a group mind.

The ultimate indicator of humanity's inclination to evolve in *Childhood's End*, however, is neither the desire for the infinite nor the ability to work in groups. It is instead—and in this Clarke seems to me truly daring—nothing less than humanity's seemingly innate desire to self-destruct. The novel opens with the fear that the Russians and the Americans may use their atomic rockets on each other, and it closes with the children of Man destroying our planet by releasing the terrific energies within the Earth's core.

In between these two moments the image that gives a form to these ideas is, interestingly enough, not the atomic bomb but the volcano. Before the Overlords arrive, Hoffman thinks to himself that his atomic rocket is about to make fires more fierce than those that first raised the island he is standing on from the Pacific depths. Later in the novel, after it has become clear that humans are not nearly so in control of Nature as they thought, Jean Greggson, the clairvoyant wife of George, has the premonition that the seemingly extinct volcano under the New Athens will "reawaken and overwhelm them all." It does, of course, but in an unexpected fashion. The people of the New Athens, realizing that their species is doomed, do as humans have been threatening to do since 1945. They use atomic weapons to reactivate the volcano; they commit mass suicide.

When the children of Man enlarge upon that explosion at the end of the novel, the destructive act becomes constructive, even nutritious; the children of Man are fed by the destroyed Earth as "a grain of wheat feeds the infant plant as it climbs towards the Sun." The human urge to end with a bang becomes the willingness to lose the self, the desire to become a piece of the continent, a part of the main.

Hindsight, then, shows that humanity was predisposed to evolve into a group consciousness. It also shows that the image of a volcano comes to stand for all the natural forces humanity—at its present stage of evolution—can neither control nor understand. When Jan Rodricks beholds, on the planet of the Overlords, a physical manifestation of the Overmind, the shape it takes, appropriately enough, is that of a volcano. The natural force that is the Overmind is about to erupt on Earth, destroying as it does so the last of humanity's illusions about its ability to control Nature.

The manifestation changes even as Rodricks looks at it. It becomes a "cyclone" and then, in the novel's penultimate scene, a "burning column" and, again, a "tornado." We become aware, as we watch, with Rodricks, Earth's last moments, that the Overmind will lead as did the pillar of fire in the desert, and that it is finally as impossible to understand as is the whirlwind in Job.

That last suggestion, that trying to understand the Overmind is like trying to hear the voice of God in a tornado, brings us back to the novel as a whole. It is not just the Overmind that is impossible to fathom, it is the future itself. What *Childhood's End* tries to do is to learn to live with the adult awareness that while the future certainly grows out of the present, it does so in ways that one of the humans in the novel finds as impossible to read as he finds the face of the chief Overlord or the eyeless gaze of one of the great stone heads on Easter Island. In fact, Clarke is able to use several of science fiction's favorite conventions to establish in the novel what might be called the ordinary expectations about several of humanity's possible futures. The invaders from outer space, for example, should be bug-eyed monsters, or humanity is destined to spread to the stars, or the last man will live out his life among the desolate cities of a devastated Earth. Clarke is then able to put against these conventional expectations unexpected revelation upon unexpected revelation. The invaders may look like devils, but they are the paternalistic Overlords. The stars are not for Man, but they are for the children of Man. The last man will live out his life on a lonely Earth, but he will also watch the race become something greater. What *Childhood's End*'s projected future projects, to put it another way, is that the future cannot be anticipated, not even by a genre as forward-looking as science fiction. Each revelation is, to be sure, a possible outgrowth of the previous action; but each revelation is so unexpected that the joy of hindsight becomes less the joy of wonder than the wonder of irony. When we look back on the conjectures of Stormgren's science-fiction-reading assistant, on his speculations about whether there may be just one Overlord ship (which turns out to be almost true), or whether the Overlords may be hiding the fact that they have nothing to hide (which turns out in a sense to be true), our response is less surprise that the assistant should guess so much than ironic awareness that the assistant cannot possibly have lived long enough to know how right and how wrong he accidentally was. Not even science fiction, in other words, can do much about the fact that humans are prisoners of their time.

What *Childhood's End* does do is to insist that the future will be so unlike the present that we would not care to live there anyway. It is not just that the Golden Age will be a long cocktail party to which we may be glad we were not invited, it is that the distant future will be as strange and inhuman-seeming as Jan Rodricks finds the children of Man. Clarke has used our adult awareness that our children are not ourselves to say that the future too will be unknowable and different from us, probably as different as is the Overmind. The future is finally, as Jan Rodricks says, beyond "optimism and pessimism alike." And because it is, we can manage not to care about not living to see very much of it.

The novel itself, however, is not beyond a certain careful optimism. It posits an end to humanity which not only fulfills to an extent our desire for a God, but which also seems to argue that all of the billions of people who have lived and died will not have lived in vain. In that the Overmind absorbs not only the children of Man but also the whole Earth and all its buried dead, the novel offers a sort of heaven, a possession of those stars which have always teased astronomer and astrologer alike with the possibility of meaning.

With the possible exception of *2001*, *Childhood's End* is the most commented-upon of Clarke's novels. The comments, not surprisingly, tend to react to the suggestion that humanity may be destined to become part of an Overmind. There are those who mention the novel's structure, its language, and even its characters; but the book is, as C. S. Lewis has said, "eschatological," and so its readers tend to by-pass such considerations —as I do—in favor of what is clearly more important to the book itself: its attitude toward what are sometimes called "the last things." As Lewis has also said, eschatological novels are not about the future in the same way as *Brave New World* is; instead, they are "speculations about the ultimate destiny of the species."

Brian Ash sees the evolution into the Overmind as a way of hoping the old-fashioned hope that "Man may be relieved from the tyranny of his own nature," that humanity may be allowed "to abandon its animal form." Josephine Hendin, using ideas more current, sees Clarke as "preoccupied with erasing the yearning 'I,' the individual discontent." He is, she says, typical of modern writers in that he assumes "that to survive well you have to be an anonymous particle, an egoless, identityless, part of the flow. The less human you are, the better chance you have to endure." It is, she explains, "a vision" of a "conceptual and emotional" alternative "to powerlessness and insecurity, to the fearfulness of our connections with other people."

Even less positive is George Edgar Slusser's insistence that the Overmind is "a parasitic vampire." In the final pages of the novel, he claims, "men become [the] Overmind," and thus cease "to feel," whereas the "Overlords learn to feel," and thus "become men." Such is, as he presents it, a nice reverse, and we do feel a certain identification with the Overlords at the end of the novel; but I cannot agree that the Overlords have only learned to feel from knowing humans, and I think we identify even more strongly with the Overmind. The latter is, after all, as Robert Scholes and Eric S. Rabkin have said, a drawing into science fiction of "some of the oldest and most potent ideas of our culture." In the Overmind, as Rabkin has said on another occasion, "we have our deepest yearnings for human importance satisfied." The novel is, as L. David Allen points out, another way of stating that "unless a man loseth his soul, he cannot gain it."

Mark Hillegas earned himself some citations in later essays when he made the mistake of using *Childhood's End* as an example of "the Baconian faith that by the systematic investigation of nature man can master the secrets of this mysterious universe and in so doing improve the human condition." The Overlords are, for Hillegas, "a manifest symbol of science," who "transform Earth into a technological Utopia where each individual can develop his potentialities to the fullest." As Thomas L. Wymer pointed out, such "is an accurate description of about the first half of the novel."

Hillegas was on his way to other points, and so is to a certain extent always quoted out of context, but his neglect of the second half of the novel is indicative of a division other readers have felt. David N. Samuelson, for example, although he has complaints about the book's structure and characters, is really most concerned about what he sees as the "sentimental mysticism," the "watered-down theological speculation," of the novel's second half. Although he acknowledges that the book has a "respect for rational thought," a sense of "cosmic perspective," a "relentless pursuit of extrapolative hypotheses," and "a genuine evocation of the sense of wonder," Samuelson argues that it is still "rooted" in the " 'respectable' British literary tradition" of Blake, the Shelleys, Morris, Wells, Stapledon, and Orwell—all of whom "wrote works in which they showed science and technology as demonic." Rather than giving "a critical appreciation of science," he says, such writers "tend to inculcate fear and hostility toward it," even, "by abdicating their function as a knowledgeable, foreseeing counterbalance," to "make more likely the technocratic state they profess to anticipate with abhorrence."

The novel has been called, then, both Baconian and Orwellian. The shift from the technological utopia achieved under the benign rule of the Overlords to the moment of evolution into the Overmind, which would seem to repudiate all of humanity's scientific achievement, has been called by Lucy Menger "a basic and logically irreconcilable thematic conflict: the power of reason vs. the power of unreason."

My own reading, I think, could be seen as an extension of Alan B. Howes' fairly carefully limited suggestion that *Childhood's End* is built of surprise twists on conventional science-fiction characters and situations. But I also agree with Menger when she goes on to say that the book speaks "to levels below the conscious mind where logical niceties do not pertain." The two halves of the novel, she argues, "have the same message: Somehow, in some form, man's lineage will cope—and survive." Scientific achievement, in other words, as the film version of *2001* so concisely shows, is just one of the stages in the race's survival. *Childhood's End* may not give "a critical appreciation of science," but it still has its own unity. As John Huntington has said:

> Clarke's myth of progress consists of two stages: that of rational, technological progress, and that of transcendent evolution. Many of his novels remain on the first stage and render technological speculations in painstaking detail. . . . But in his most far-reaching novels technological progress fails to satisfy, and mankind advances, not by inventing more competent machinery, but by mutating into a higher form of being. This transcendental vision offers, not the detailed ingenuity of mechanical invention, but powerful hints of modes of understanding and perception and of mental powers and controls that so completely surpass those we ourselves experience that they are incomprehensible to us.

6

Harry Purvis

IN the mid-1950s, in places as diverse as Miami, London, and Sydney, Clarke wrote a series of what he called "tall" tales, stories in which both the science and the fiction are exaggerated to the very edge of any possible suspension of disbelief. The stories feature, among other things, a biologist who is trying to prepare termites to inherit the Earth; the accidental discovery of anti-gravity, which leads, ironically, not to a flight but to a fall; and an exasperated husband who pushes his domineering wife out of a fourth-story window, ostensibly because she talks too much, but really because she has an unscientific attitude.

What one remembers about the collection of these tales, which is called *Tales from the White Hart* (1957), is not so much the exaggeration of the science or the fiction, but the attitude of the taleteller. The globe-trotting and perhaps homesick Clarke re-created the cozy, all-male world of a Fleet Street pub, and in it, on Wednesday evenings, a fine storyteller, one Harry Purvis, B.Sc. ("at least"), Ph.D. ("probably"), F.R.S. (probably not, "though it has been rumoured"), shares with us one "top secret" tale after another.

Moreover, while it is true that in these stories inventors are regularly blown up by their inventions, which was the great fear of the 1950s, it is also true that in each story, the voice of Purvis, the audacity of his put-downs and his self-possession, becomes for us the audacity of humanity itself, the sheer gall and even perversity (Purvis-ity) of our trying either to know or to do anything in the face of—or the nonface of—the universe's great silence.

At the beginning of one of the stories, "The Ultimate Melody," Clarke, who includes himself in these tales as a member of Purvis' audience, notes that there are moments, even in crowded rooms, when all conversations seem to stop at once, when there is "a sudden, vibrating emptiness that seems to swallow up all sound." Such moments, he says, are "as if everybody is listening for something"; in his case for "Time's wingéd chariot." Such moments, he seems to mean, put him in mind, not only of his own sure and coming end, but also of the great silence that—it is predicted—will one day swallow up humanity and all of the noises it has ever made.

Against such a depressing thought comes the voice of Harry Purvis, not just in this story but in all the stories, telling of some human's presumptuous attempt to conquer the environment, to invent something that will increase the dominance of humans over Nature. The attempts always fail, or at best have not yet succeeded; but we cannot but treasure, as do Harry's listeners in the pub, the audacity of such whistling in the dark. It is not "the ultimate melody," but it is a brave attempt to hope that the evidence is not yet complete, that humanity may still be able to postpone for ages and ages yet its disappearance into the great silence.

In some of these stories, as in much of his early fiction, Clarke seems to fear that humans will use their science to turn their backs on this unsympathetic-seeming universe. Just as Richard Peyton III, in the tower of Comarre, dreams that he dwells on a beautiful beach, caught up in the forgetfulness of a perfect love, oblivious alike to the other worlds suggested by the stars overhead and to the coming destruction prophesied by the waves on the beach, so in these stories much is made of the possibility of creating dream worlds by feeding artificial sensations directly to the brain, of creating personal cities of Diaspar.

In "Patent Pending" a scientist invents a machine that can record and play back—even for another—the brain waves of a person having an intense experience. The scientist's assistant, a young entrepreneur, decides to record the brain waves of a gourmet at his favorite meal, and of a prostitute and her apache (the last named, appropriately enough it seems, Hercule). The assistant has, not surprisingly, no difficulty finding businessmen willing to market the results.

The brain-wave machine is, as one of Purvis' hearers interrupts to say, borrowed from the "feelies" in *Brave New World*. The scientist's assistant, for that matter, is called Dupin, a name Clarke may have taken from Poe's detective of that name (the latter does, after all, spend as much time as he can in darkened rooms, trying to keep exterior reality from interfering with the life in his mind). But the point is that Clarke's Dupin is as doomed as is the Huxley-like future society of Diaspar. The scientist's assistant is not able to refrain from sampling his own wares, from enjoying himself as Hercule in the arms of Susette the professional; and so the story ends, as such stories are supposed to, especially if they are set in France, with Clarke's Dupin shot dead by his *petite dame*. The woman is convinced, as well she might be, that her man is in love with another; she becomes exterior reality, which reasserts itself by destroying the dreamer.

Similarly, in the story already mentioned, "The Ultimate Melody," after a computer has been used to analyze hundreds of popular melodies in an effort to find the fundamental one, the basic tune to which all other unforgettable melodies are but approximations, the computer's programmer is driven mad by the tune the machine isolates. The fundamental melody turns out to be so matched to the electrical patterns in the human brain that the computer programmer will have to spend the rest of his days short-circuited, caught up in a trance by a melody he cannot forget. He loses "all consciousness of the outer world."

A member of Purvis' audience suggests that the computer programmer has found "the ultimate reality that philosophers like Plato are always talking about." If so, the story says that the reality so found is destructive. Plato argued that ultimate reality is to be found by examining closely the ideas in the mind, but other evidence certainly suggests that looking inward for the ultimate reality is like trying to hear the melody beneath all the melodies that stick in one's head. The ultimate reality to be found by looking inward is the movement of electrical forces in the brain, and to focus on those is to turn away from the larger realities of the universe, is to surrender oneself to the elements.

The more immediate danger to the human race, however, as Purvis' stories see it, is the attitude toward existence embodied by the character Aunt Henrietta in the story "The Reluctant Orchid." There, an "inoffensive little clerk" tries to murder his loud-mouthed and overbearing aunt by feeding her to a giant meat-eating orchid. The story climaxes when Aunt Henrietta—who, in addition to wearing "a rather loud line in Harris tweeds," driving a Jaguar "with reckless skill," and chain-smoking cigars, raises very large dogs—tames the carnivorous plant. The taming does not take much; one sight of Aunt Henrietta standing there, "arms akimbo," and the orchid whips its tentacles, not around her, but protectively *"around itself."* "I'm used to animals," she says. "You must treat them firmly—but gently. Kindness always works, as long as you show them you're the master."

The story is, then, a Thurber-like confrontation of timid male and domineering female, one which ends with the male discovering that his plans can go as a-gley as those of any

mouse. But the interesting point is that at the end of the story
Aunt Henrietta remains as disquieting to the reader as she was
in the beginning. We might agree that it is poetic justice that
the ultimate result of her being able to tame the plant is that
her nephew, whom she continues to dominate, becomes more
and more like a plant himself; but the disquieting thing is that
through it all Henrietta remains untouched, unaware of the
animosity she has aroused in her nephew and of the wider
implications of her philosophy of showing Nature who is boss.
The entire focus of the story is less on the nephew getting his
comeuppance than on Henrietta's continuing to be cheerful
—a hardy fellow well met with a "booming voice" and a
"bone-crushing" handshake. In the context of the rest of
Purvis' tales, such a character can be seen as dangerous,
finally as embodying an attitude that is immediately threatening to the existence of the race. The story is Clarke's version of
Wells' "The Flowering of the Strange Orchid," the latter a
story of an orchid fancier who almost falls victim to a blood-
sucking plant; but Clarke's story suggests that the attitude
which assumes that humanity is the master of the universe,
that Nature is only a reluctant dragon, is more immediately
dangerous than any threat from Nature.

Several of Purvis' stories have, as an example of the fear
that humanity may be as overconfident as is Aunt Henrietta,
the Cold War fear that the race may blow itself up. This fear,
which Clarke touched upon in his early stories, and which we
have seen as the motive behind both *Earthlight* and *Childhood's End*, is, in Purvis' tales, part of the more general fear
that humanity may have put too much faith in its place in the
universe, may trust too much that its science will see it
through.

It is one thing, after all, to look back with nostalgia to more
innocent days, as does Purvis in the story "Moving Spirit."
There he tells us about a rich and eccentric inventor who
accidentally causes an explosion when he tries to age his

homemade whiskey electronically. We are reminded, when we see the inventor draped over a beam in his barn, of the essentially good-humored explosion that attended the making of Cavorite in Wells' *The First Men in the Moon*. The only militarily threatening result of the explosion in Purvis' story is that the commander of the local Home Guard wants to equip his troops with what the inventor has called, in order to avoid being prosecuted for making whiskey illegally, his Osmotic Bomb, what might be called his attempt to harness the force that through the green fuse drives the sap.

It is quite another thing, in the middle of the decade when the atomic bomb first seemed to threaten the untimely arrival of the great silence, to tell stories with titles such as "Cold War" and "Armaments Race." While it is true that the original action of the first, the hiring of a retired submarine commander by the state of California to land a phony iceberg on a Florida beach, is harmless enough, that action is finally seen against the background of a Russian submarine trying to steal the downed nose cone of an American missile. And in "Armaments Race," a movie special-effects man, who is trying to design a real-looking death-ray, does in fact design a real death-ray. The tone of both stories is light, but in both humanity seems unable to avoid competition, to avoid playing at war. In both, the titles seem almost tension relievers, hopes that neither the Cold War nor the armaments race will result in anything more serious than a prank or entertainment. Gone are the innocent explosions of yesteryear; in both of these stories, as in other impossible and self-defeating situations, we laugh that we might not cry.

Two of Purvis' stories even go so far as to entertain the possibility that science itself may just be evidence of humanity's tendency to overreach. "Big Game Hunt" is about trying to control, with electrical impulses, larger and larger animals, and it climaxes with a giant squid reaching up and pulling a boatload of scientists into the depths. The monster is described

—appropriately enough, by a passage out of *Moby Dick*—as having "innumerable long arms radiating from its center, curling and twisting like a nest of anacondas." The humans in the boat, like Ahab before them, fall victim to an enraged and finally uncontrollable representative of Nature.

"What Goes Up," as the title implies, is about an inevitable fall. When a scientist, whom Purvis calls Dr. Cavor in honor of Wells' character of that name, happens, while trying to control atomic energy, to create a giant sphere of anti-gravity, he finds that to reach the reactor at the center of the sphere he has to use the same amount of energy it would take to lift him free of Earth, to raise him "*four thousand miles* against the steady drag of normal gravity." When he slips, as of course he must, his fall is as if from a "four-thousand-mile-high mountain"; it is, because as if from beyond Earth's gravity, exactly as if he had fallen "from the remotest stars."

"Ah, what a fall was there, my countrymen," says Purvis, as well he might. Even though the fall comes at the end of what is, even for Purvis, an outrageous string of truth-stretchers, it is still linked with the falls of other human overreachers. Purvis winds up comparing his Dr. Cavor, not to Wells' reasonably successful scientist, but to Mary Shelley's unsuccessful one (he speaks of "Dr. Cavor's Frankensteinian fall"). Such a linking hints that Purvis sometimes fears that humanity itself will slip while reaching for the stars.

The unhappy relationship that sometimes seems to exist between humans and their science is epitomized by Purvis' version of "Sleeping Beauty" and the twists he works on that old story. He tells us about Sigmund Snoring, a young man with the unfortunate habit of living up to his last name. To cure his problem, Sigmund is given a drug which keeps him awake all of the time. For Sigmund, however, life does not seem capable of filling all those extra hours; he gets to the point where he cannot "read another book, go to another nightclub, or listen to another gramaphone record." So he visits again the story's fairy godmother, the scientist who gave him the drug, and is given another drug, this time one which puts him to sleep so soundly that he cannot be awakened. The scientist had not meant to reverse Sigmund's situation so drastically, but before he can do anything about it, he has his own Frankensteinian failure: he is bitten by an irate guinea pig, gets blood poisoning, and dies. Sigmund, then, is allowed to sleep on, in part because his wife is tired of him and wants to live on his money, but also because the story seems to want to wonder whether science is the fairy godmother we have taken it to be. The wife may one day consent to allow other scientists to try to waken Sigmund, but the story ends with science having overreached again. Sigmund may wake to a new life, even to a new world as does the central character in Wells' *When the Sleeper Wakes*, but Purvis' story stops well short of saying so.

In fact, two of the most positive stories in the collection can only manage to argue that the human race may not have lived in vain.

"The Pacifist" argues that the scientists of the world may begin to consider the wider implications of their work, may refuse to cooperate with the generals of the world. A scientist, whom Purvis calls Dr. Milquetoast (even though he admits that the man has a "stubborn streak" beneath his "mild and diffident exterior"), finally programs a computer to reply to all questions of a military nature by calling the general who asks such questions a "pompous baboon," thus insisting that the military mind has not evolved enough to appreciate the implications of atomic warfare.

Even if scientists do not refuse to cooperate, says Purvis, computers are getting almost smart enough "to disobey us without any Milquetoast interfering with their circuits." "When that happens," he concludes, "we'll just have to say to the dinosaurs: 'Move over a bit—here comes *homo sap*!' And the transistor shall inherit the Earth." The products of our science, ironically enough, will be wise enough to do as we should have done, to save themselves from the misuse of that science.

Similarly, in "The Next Tenants," a biology professor, a Japanese who lost his family at Nagasaki, is dedicating his life to giving tools to termites in the hope of preparing them to inherit the Earth. It is not that the professor hates humanity; he just fears that its days are numbered and wants "to save something from the wreckage." Like the alien visitor in several of Clarke's early stories—and in *2001*—the professor has given the termites the lever and the sledge, and is about to give them fire. He announces this intention on a Pacific atoll, "not a thousand miles from Bikini," and as he does so, Purvis, who claims to have talked to the professor himself, becomes aware of the sunset, that it is "partly of man's making," that it is a sign that at that very moment "Teller and his team [have] started the hydrogen reaction." The question in the story becomes whether termites will be able to do anything more with the gift of fire than did humanity. "I think we should give them the chance," says Purvis, resolving not to give away the exact location of the professor's experiment.

If the Earth is to be inherited by machines or by educated insects, then it is possible to conclude that the race which built the machines or educated the insects has not itself lived in vain. But it is not quite the role we imagined for ourselves in the days before the Cold War, and it is at best only more meaningful-seeming than is the pointless passing of the dinosaurs.

Which brings me around again to Aunt Henrietta, or really to her other self, Ermintrude Inch, the antagonist in the one story Clarke seems to have written especially for this collection, "The Defenestration of Ermintrude Inch." The Inches, Osbert and Ermintrude, disagree about how much Ermintrude talks. They do agree to test the matter by installing a word-counter, a machine which can separate deep and high tones and thus keep track of how many words each speaks. The first experiment gives Osbert an easy victory, but the second time he tries it, he discovers to his shocked disbelief that his word count far exceeds that of his very talkative wife. What he also discovers, however, when he looks into the matter, is that Ermintrude has used a tape recording of his voice to up his score. The result of this discovery is the defenestration of Mrs. Inch.

The fact that Osbert then marries "a charming little deaf-and-dumb girl," and that they are, according to Purvis, one of the "happiest couples" he knows, suggests that Osbert got rid of Ermintrude in order to restore silence to his life. But the story as a whole makes it clear that Osbert shoved Ermintrude out the window because she cheated on the experiment, because she had no respect for scientific inquiry.

Ermintrude becomes, then, the representative of all the unscientific people in these stories; she stands for the scientist's assistant who wants to make money out of the recordings of people's most intense emotional experiences, for the general who wants Milquetoast's computer to fight his wars for him, for Aunt Henrietta who does not realize the implications of her unthinking attempts to dominate the world around her. And when Osbert pushes Ermintrude out the window, his act becomes the one time in the collection (other than Dr. Milquetoast) when the timid souls who have been too involved in their research to notice how their work is being misused all fight back.

Unfortunately, just as Purvis finishes the story, his wife, Mrs. Purvis, bursts into the pub and carries Harry off, scolding him as she goes. It is the first (and last) time Harry's friends have seen Mrs. Purvis, who is described as being a large and "formidable" blonde, and they do not know whether the "Very well, Ermintrude" he was heard to say as he was hauled off was a slip of the tongue or in fact her name. They only know that they have not seen Harry since.

The story of the defenestration of Ermintrude Inch is, then, another Walter Mitty-ish daydream. Clarke, who has himself remained single after a brief marriage, and whose novels feature few enough women, has drawn upon the long and irony-laden tradition of antifeminism to embody for this collection the misuse of science. He has used the picture that shows the domineering woman as combining the worst of both sexes, a picture shared by men as far from each other in time as Thurber and the Wife of Bath's fifth husband, to capture the race's unnatural urge to self-destruct. And even though all the misusers of science in these tales are not women by any means, still, in such a tradition, where all of the people of good heart are too timid to act, the hope that scientists will revolt becomes no more likely than that Walter Mitty could really fix an artificial lung with a piece from a borrowed fountain pen.

The tone of the collection, taken as a whole, is fairly represented by the story of "The Man Who Ploughed the Sea," and by the fact that Purvis bids us "good night" at the end of almost every story. "The Man Who Ploughed the Sea" is prefaced by a reference to the White Hart's landlord having to shout that it is "Time, gentlemen, *pleeze!*" before he can force his patrons "out into the cold hard world." It is about men who have founded their own companies, who have made great fortunes from their expertise and wield great power because of their money. But it has, at its center, a man whose days are numbered, who, in spite of his knowledge, money, and power, has but a year to live. He has invented a way of mining the sea, but he cannot possibly live long enough to perfect it. He gives up the idea to others, sets sail in a yacht, and is finally buried at sea. The story concludes with Purvis reflecting that the man, who was a "fanatical conservationist," surely would have appreciated the fact that his own atoms may one day be mined by his own process. For that matter, says Purvis, just before he bids us good night, since "everything goes back to the sea in the long run," "it's only a matter of time before . . . all of us" make some such "contribution" to the future. Harry's good night is more than just a good wish; it is a reminder that time runs out, that it is a cold hard world, that in spite of the greatest technology the world has ever known, in spite of power that staggers the imagination, for all of us the bird of time is on the wing and has but a little way to go.

Purvis' reflections are about the end of the race, and they draw their power, as such reflections always do, from our own coming ends. But there is still a limited hope in these tales told in the White Hart, a hope that draws its power, oddly enough, from the very idea of the great silence.

The thing to look back on is the fact that Osbert Inch wanted to restore silence to his life. It is fairly daring of Clarke, in a collection of tales that has in its background the fear that humanity may be rushing into the great silence, to have one of the characters succeed in making silence by pushing another out of a window. It turns out that the removal of Ermintrude is only a wish, but the making of silence is still a daring suggestion in a collection in which the thing most wrong with Aunt Henrietta and Ermintrude is that they are too busy making noise to hear the threat of silence.

In the first story of the volume, "Silence Please," an inventor makes a machine that can cancel out all sound within a given area. The machine is used in the story by a rejected lover (not the inventor) to cancel out the sound of an opera in which his ex-beloved is singing. In that the opera plot is a particularly awful version of a love triangle, the actual use of the machine may be paralleled to trying to keep Aunt Henrietta and Ermintrude quiet enough to hear the silence, the suggestion being that we are too involved in our petty jealousies and competitions to be aware of the danger to all of us when such lovers' quarrels are raised to the national level.

But the really interesting thing about this story depends upon the fact that the machine blows up at the end, taking its inventor with it. Such might be just another statement of the failure of science, except that Purvis remarks of the explosion that at least the inventor "perished in the moment of achievement." And he prefaces the tale with a line very like that curious last line of Mary Shelley's Victor Frankenstein, the line which says that what I have failed at, another may do. Purvis says that "one day—who knows?—someone may perfect [the silencer] and earn the blessings of the world."

Unless we are to assume that Purvis means that we may come to bless the invention of the atomic bomb because it may end the race—a position much more pessimistic than anything either he or Clarke has ever hinted at—we have to assume that the making of silence in this case is a good, that there is something in the control of a small part of the great silence that is somehow hopeful—however slightly—to humanity.

The same thing has to be said about Purvis' ability to make silence with his stories, to stun his audience into having nothing to say. At the end of "Silence Please," for example, when he is asked why no one has ever heard of this silencer, he says that, under the circumstances, it was thought "highly appropriate to—ah—*hush* the whole business up." The double reference is so dreadful that it really leaves Harry's detractors nothing to say.

The story that makes the most sense of this use of the power to create silence is the most hopeful story in the book, a story about an apparent danger which turns out not to be real, at least not this time: "Critical Mass."

The story takes place, as Purvis sets the scene, in a little inn in rural England, a pub where the customers are a mixture of locals and of scientists from the nearby and recently constructed Atomic Energy Research Establishment. The relationship between the two groups is friendly enough, but it includes "a certain amount of half-serious leg-pulling." The scientists are always being asked what they are going "to blow up next."

On the day to which Purvis calls our attention, the innkeeper opines that sooner or later the scientists are going "to let out something" they "won't be able to bottle up again." "And *then* where will we be?" he asks.

"Half-way to the Moon," the chief scientist replies, a bit tired of such questions. The locals take him to mean an explosion that will blow up the whole countryside, but the reply also argues, of course, that whatever the dangers of science, it also has the power that may allow humans to examine the reality beyond their world.

The story does not take up this second meaning directly; instead, it describes the wreck of a truck from the Research Establishment, the sight—seen from the inn window—of the truck driver seeming to flee for his life, and the fear that there is going to be an explosion. The mysterious substance seen to be leaking like a gas from the truck's cargo turns out on closer inspection to be bees, trying to return to their broken hives; but Purvis admits that he wondered all of the way from the inn to the truck whether he and his scientist friends were not like the military commander on the volcanic island who kept insisting that there was not any danger, right up to the moment when the volcano blew up and took the island with it. Purvis knew what sort of research was being done at the Establishment, and that the truck could not possibly be carrying anything explosive, but the panic of the local residents undermined his certainty. This time it turns out that science can—or at least that an apiarist can—bottle up again what has been turned loose. But it is responsible of Purvis to worry, and the story has a definite sense of relief that his worry turns out to be as needless as his reason told him it should be. It is possible that the human race may self-destruct; but it is also possible that reason will prevail, that humans may use their science to help them escape from the prison of this single world.

All of which brings me to why Purvis' friends miss him so. They have not, as I said, seen him since the evening his wife appeared and carried him off, and they miss him. They want him to do anything he has to do to return, even if it means defenestrating Ermintrude. They want him to come and tell them more stories, even stories that repeat what they already know: that it is a dark and deadly world out there beyond the walls of their cozy pub. What they want is the slight and almost perverse suggestion that we may be able to control the onset of silence, may be able to find ourselves halfway to the Moon without having been blown up.

7

Not Yet the Stars

THE copyright page of *Childhood's End* carries the interesting disclaimer that "the opinions expressed in this book are not those of the author." Clarke has written to me that because he had just published *The Exploration of Space*, a nonfiction work which argues that the stars *are* for Man, he wanted to "disassociate" himself from the opposite opinion, which is expressed in the novel. "It was as simple as that," he writes, but then adds: "except that nothing is that simple."

And nothing is. It is difficult to believe, and Clarke does not say, that any author could suffer the pains of writing a book the opinions of which he does not in some sense accept. As I have already said, *Childhood's End* seems to me a product of its time, an argument that even in the midst of the Cold War one might hope that our species is not simply suicidal, that in some sense the stars still are for Man. The book is even, I think, a somewhat daring claim that humanity's apparent urge to self-destruct might be turned into an affirmation of some of our oldest and most cherished beliefs about ourselves and our place in the universe.

It further seems to me that if we look back at *Childhood's End* from the novels Clarke has written since then, it becomes more and more difficult to see any opinion in that novel which he does not still agree with. *Childhood's End* may be something of a desperate overstatement—a sort of How long, O Lord, how long?—but if we discount that, if we say that the immediate evolution into the Overmind is a kind of overstatement, a claim produced by what Clarke has called (in *A Fall of Moondust*) "that psychotic era, the Frantic Fifties," then it can become clear that in the novels since then Clarke, having weathered the Cold War with the desperate optimism of *Childhood's End* and the careful and very limited optimism of Harry Purvis, has continued to hope, however cautiously, that there is some truth in our ancient view of ourselves as somehow important, as somehow capable of coming to grips with a larger part of the universe. The hope is phrased in various ways, but it is still there.

The Deep Range (1957) is set in the not-too-distant future, on an Earth that has universal education, a world-wide democracy, and that farms the seas so successfully that humanity need "never be hungry again." The book is about a man, Walter Franklin, who has had to resign from the space program and settle for life in that other alien environment, the sea. It features the discovery, on Franklin's part, that the sea can give him a goal in life; the sighting of the Great Sea Serpent, which proves that the sea still has its secrets; and even a love story, one not unrelated to the novel's larger themes. But it is, at the end, about getting the human race ready for space, about becoming worthy of the stars.

The action takes place largely underwater, in that inhospitable world inhabited by Professor Sullivan in *Childhood's End*. The book spends much time hunched over the control panels of one-man submarines, watching the game wardens of the future as they herd the whales across the ocean ranges. The only stars these humans contemplate are those on the boards before them, the green lights of their instruments and the images on their sonar screens. They keep themselves alive, however, as do people in space, by protecting themselves with machines. And the central character has the fear of space evident in *Childhood's End*, the "astrophobia" that is one of the reasons the race does not seem ready for the stars.

Walter Franklin had, while he was a spaceman, the terrifying experience of being adrift in a spacesuit, his controls jammed, his radio broken, and his ship out of sight. All he had was "the knowledge that there was space all around him, all the way out to the stars." Since then he has been subject to "the terror of those endless, trackless wastes between the worlds." Even on Earth he can feel the planet "whirling faster and faster on its axis, trying to hurl him off like a stone from a sling." Hold as he will to whatever is solid around him, "the endless fall" can seem to begin again.

The cure for Franklin's fear of space turns out to be both the somewhat motherly embrace of the woman who has come to love him and the sense of kinship he develops, not only with other human beings, but with all the creatures of the sea, even those he has to kill.

When he is racked by the attack of fear just described, Franklin grovels in the sand and weeps "like a heartbroken child." His future wife, who has already been attracted by his looking "lost and more than a little worried," crosses the "line between compassion and love" and embraces "his heaving shoulders." She comforts him by saying that he will be all right, that "there's nothing to be afraid of."

That same evening, in despair of ever being cured, Franklin tries to commit suicide by allowing a diving torpedo to pull him to depths where no human can survive. He gives himself, "a willing sacrifice, gladly into the grasp of the great mother of life"; he seeks the "blissful euphoria" of "oblivion" instead of the pain of continuing to live. But he is embraced again, this time by a rugged individualist, an outlaw submariner who leads illegal hunting parties into the world's underwater preserves. The businessmen who are along on the illegal expedition are at first reluctant to risk their lives to save a game warden, but finally they agree that they have to go outside the sub and "fetch that guy in." Franklin had seen, just before he lost consciousness, a "galaxy" of lights from small sea creatures flash and be gone, and he had told himself that the Milky Way "was of no longer duration, of no greater importance, when seen against the background of eternity." And it is perhaps so. But Franklin survives to find that, whatever the ultimate truth about the cosmos, he has been rescued by other humans, that instead of the separateness of outer space he is surrounded by a web of interrelationships which, like the "continuous and sustaining fluid" of the sea, can give him back "the sense of security he lost in space."

Several incidents in the novel seem to suggest that Clarke was afraid that Franklin's physical courage, or the lack of it, might become an issue for the reader. By the end of the book, the former spaceman has on more than one occasion demonstrated his ability to function in dangerous situations in an environment as immediately deadly as outer space. In fact, Franklin's penultimate action is, while dressed only in a diving suit, to rescue a trapped submarine. At the time he is as alone as he was in outer space (and really in more danger), and the incident is surely meant to be a reverse of the moment when the people inside the poacher's sub risked their lives to save his.

But the real issue of courage in the book is whether Franklin has the moral strength, after he has become chief of his bureau, to say publicly that he and the majority of other wardens think that the time has come to stop killing whales. The question becomes whether the race—as represented by Franklin—can manage to acknowledge a kinship, not just within a family of other humans, but with all the other living beings with which we share this planet. As the Maha Thero, the Buddhist leader, puts it late in the novel: "Since the beginning of history . . . man has assumed that the other animals exist only for his benefit." The time has come, since "the production of all types of synthetic protein from purely vegetable sources is now an economic possibility," to ask whether the killing, which "is no longer essential," should not "cease." "Within a generation," says the Thero, "we can shed the burden of guilt which, however lightly or heavily it has weighed on individual consciences, must at some time or other have haunted all thinking men as they look at the world of life which shares their planet."

Franklin passes the test of moral courage, and our agreement with him is carefully prepared for. From the first the whales are clearly very smart. They seem to know immediately when a warden has killed a great shark that was attacking the herd. They certainly have some sort of language, and they are better at the use of sonar than are the humans within their subs. All wardens come to know "a kinship with all the creatures" of the sea, even with those it is their "duty to destroy," but, above all, they feel "a sympathy and an almost mystical reverence . . . towards the great beasts whose destinies [they rule]." When Franklin, seated in a small boat, approaches two killer whales, both rear their heads out of the water and stare "at him with their huge, intelligent eyes." "The unusual attitude" gives him "the uncanny impression" that he is "face to face not with animals but with beings who might be higher in the order of creation than himself."

Franklin tries to dismiss that idea by reminding himself that the species of whale he is looking at is "the most ruthless killer in the seas." But he has to admit, upon reflection, that the killer whale is only "the second most ruthless killer." The most ruthless is, of course, humanity, and we are set up for that admission from the beginning. "There was a killer loose on the

range," says the book's opening sentence, and although the
killer turns out to be a shark, the warden and his sub which set
out after it are described as even more dangerous, as "more
deadly than any other creature that [roams] the seas." All of
which is confirmed by the giant slaughterhouses, which are
described in some detail, where whales are killed and butch-
ered very efficiently.

"Don't you think whales are in a different class?" one of the
minor characters asks Franklin, "half apologetically." But
Franklin has been coming around to that opinion since the
moment when he first found himself afloat in his sub in the
midst of a whale herd. He realized even then, not only that he
and a nearby whale were both mammals, but that he was a
"biped who had abandoned the sea" and the other was a
"quadruped who had returned to it."

Franklin is not by nature a reflective man; he cannot, for
example, quite make out the "connection" between his own
attempt at suicide and his later objections to killing other creatures. He cannot see that the latter is in part the result of the
shared sense of life he got from being rescued. But his instincts
are good. He knows that there is some reason why he is reminded, that first time he is amidst the whales, of "the moment
when [as a spaceman] he had first seen Earth, in all its heart-
stopping beauty, floating against the infinitely distant background of the stars." Both scenes, we realize, imply kinship in
a universe that seems otherwise lonely.

The idea that it is time to quit killing at least the higher
animals is introduced into the novel by the Maha Thero, but it
is anticipated in other ways. The researchers of Franklin's
bureau, for example, have made an aquarium where "surprising partnerships" have developed, where creatures that are
ordinarily enemies in "the endlessly turning wheel of life and
death" are managing to live in the same cages. It is "a peaceful
little world," very "different from the battlefield of the reef."
Were the lab staff to fail "to make the normal feeding arrange-

ments," the "harmony would quickly vanish"; but in the pool, as with the whales at the end of the novel, humans have made a "start" at imposing a "truce upon the battlefield of Nature." As one of the scientists, who is trying to train killer whales into something like sheep dogs, asks Franklin: "If science and religion can combine to take some of the cruelty out of Nature, isn't it a good thing?"

The novel concludes with Walter Franklin watching his son begin a career as a spaceman, the profession he had to give up in his own youth. Franklin is not saddened by the experience; he has had his own other world to explore, and he can, as do others of Clarke's protagonists, feel a sense of kinship with those future generations who will voyage to the stars. But such an ending to the novel does widen the circle of kinship even farther. The Maha Thero has said to Franklin, as part of the argument against killing whales, that "sooner or later we will meet types of intelligent life much higher than our own, yet in forms completely alien. And when that time comes, the treatment man receives from his superiors may well depend upon the way he has behaved toward the other creatures of his own world." It is, to be sure, an argument that would appeal to a former spaceman; but Franklin remembers it as he watches his son's spaceship disappear into the sky, and he whispers to the stars that suddenly seem very close: "Give us another hundred years . . . and we'll face you with clean hands and hearts—whatever shape you be."

Franklin had, after he first heard the shrieks and squeals whales make to each other, nightmares of goblins and demon-haunted forests. But "weirdness lies only in unfamiliarity," and he has grown fond of these enormous animals who make such falsetto screams. There is, however, a memory still evoked when he sits in his sub listening to the sounds in the sea, a memory of sitting in the radio rooms of spaceships listening, not only to the noises of "man's feeble transmitters," but to "the endless susurration of the stars and galaxies themselves as they drenched the whole universe with radiation." The novel wants to hope that the sense of kinship will widen to include that immensity.

A Fall of Moondust (1961) is really a version of the mine-disaster story. A tourist boat sinks into a sea of dust on the Moon, and the novel is about the relationships inside the buried vehicle and the attempts outside to find and then to rescue them. The story is neatly done, and Clarke manages the alternations of hope and despair in workmanlike fashion.

The book has the usual consequences of such stories. The people trapped underground demonstrate remarkable courage and togetherness, the young lovers discover each other, and the captain of the boat becomes a man. In fact, the captain, having observed that "the petty dross of selfishness and cowardice" has been "burned out" of his passengers by their "encounter with death," wonders if the real reason people seek danger is not that "only thus" can they "find the companionship and solidarity" they "unconsciously" crave.

Be that as it may, the novel certainly insists that the people are rescued by other people; by people working together, in spite of individual personality clashes, to come up with a technological solution to the death-threatening situation. There is no moment of prayer on the tourist boat, no sudden revelation of faith; there is only the hope that the skill and knowledge of the engineers on the surface of the sea of dust can come up with a workable plan. The trapped people are waiting for messages from above, but what they want to hear is the sound of probes touching the roof of their boat, the exploratory mechanical finger of other humans, not of God.

The novel has an interesting focus on the struggle for existence generally. The engineers and scientists who are out to rescue the trapped people have long held pictures of themselves as locked in a battle with Nature. The scientist who is also a priest, who believes in God as well as Man, comes up with the wrong answer and causes a delay in the rescue attempt. The scientist who works out a way of locating the boat is an unlikable but dedicated fellow, one who has always seen himself as in a "fight" with "the Universe." The engineer who carries out the actual rescue has a history of pitting "his wits against this strange and beautiful world"; he sees this attempt as "the greatest battle of his life."

We get an interesting perspective on the battle between humanity and Nature if we juxtapose it to the thoughts of one of the tourists in the boat, a Mr. Radley, who is convinced, not only that flying saucers exist and have been visiting Earth for thousands of years, but that "the forces of good and evil are at war in the Universe, just as they are on Earth." Such thinking, we are told by one of the trustworthy characters in the novel, is left over from "the Frantic Fifties," that time in "the mid-twentieth century" when "a substantial percentage of the population was convinced that the world was about to be destroyed, and that the only hope lay in intervention from space." "Having lost faith in themselves," we are told, humans "sought salvation from the sky."

We know from *Childhood's End* that Clarke himself had a touch of the mid-century loss of faith, though he qualified it even then by saying that the opinions in the book were not his. But Radley has to become for us something more than a simple clown. He is a clown; it turns out he thinks the sinking of the tour boat was an effort of the saucerians to get rid of him because he knows too much. His is an overstated view of himself at the center of the cosmos. But his vision of existence as a struggle is not repudiated by the book. If anything, it is almost affirmed. The battle is not seen as a battle between good and evil; it is seen as an attempt by humanity to stave off destruction and to win a greater share of the universe.

At the moment when the tour boat is sinking, the captain has a sudden recall of a moment on a beach when he was a boy. He remembers "a tiny pit, perfectly smooth and symmetrical," and "something lurking in its depths—something completely buried except for its waiting jaws." It was an ant lion, and the captain feels as "helpless," as his boat slides down into the dust, as the "doomed insect he had watched so many years ago."

The captain knows that no malevolent beast dug the pit into which they have fallen, but his whole experience under the dust is filled with times when he has to wonder "if there might be something in Radley's delusion." At a time of despair late in the novel, he feels "for the first time in his life . . . an emotion of sheer, overwhelming hate," for the dust from which they seem unable to escape. It seems to him that the "Sea of Thirst," the name of the dust bowl into which they have sunk, is "a conscious, malignant entity" that has "been playing with them like a cat with a mouse." "Perhaps," he says to himself, "Radley [is] right, after all."

At the actual moment of escape, the captain, who is the last one up a rope ladder before the boat fills with the rising dust, feels "as if a million soft yet determined fingers" are "clutching at him, pulling him back into the rising flood." The Sea of Thirst seems to relax "its grip on him" only "slowly" and "reluctantly." As he looks back from safety, he sees the dust "rising swiftly behind him, still un-rippled, still smooth and placid—and inexorable." At such a moment, in a novel in which a television cameraman can see the stake marking the location of the sunken boat as a symbol of "the loneliness of man in this huge and hostile universe that he [is] attempting to conquer," it is impossible not to see the captain's escape as a symbol of humanity staying just a step ahead of annihilation.

During the ordeal under the dust, the captain and the boat's stewardess, who have been attracted to each other, slip away into the air lock and get to know each other—in both "the literal and the Biblical sense." They have not planned things that way, but the proximity and the threat of death overwhelm them. Instinctively, we are told, their bodies know "that, in the long run, love [is] the only defense against death."

By the end of the novel the captain and the stewardess have

married, and she is pregnant with that future human life which is, written large, the race's only defense against extermination. But the book is in a hesitant way even more optimistic than that. The captain, who had been "a competent but unambitious youngster," has, because his beloved Moon has tried to kill him, decided to become a space pilot. His job on the Moon seems to him a dead end in more ways than one, and he has decided that he, like his race, must go beyond.

Such a decision is more convincing in the light of the novel as a whole. We have to see the captain as discovering that the "programmed course" of his life, like that of his boat, can lead but to the grave.

So, of course, may venturing into space. But as the captain thinks to himself, although deep space may be "still more hostile and unforgiving," he does not as yet see it as having "declared war on him." In the middle of the Sea of Thirst, because the horizon on the Moon is so close, the dust can seem to stretch to the stars; it can seem to roll "onward beneath the stars" "for ever and ever." But that sight is an "illusion"; the sea of dust does end, and it is just possible that the end to the race that the dust suggests, the "inexorable" rising surface which threatens to bury us all, may also be an illusion. "There may be *anything* up in those hills," says the stewardess of some unexplored lunar mountains; "we simply don't know." Nor do we know what, if any, alternatives may be represented by those stars that stand out against "a blackness so complete that the mind [rebels] against it." Such a hope is "beyond logic or reason," as in the desire of the trapped people to die like humans rather than like animals; but so is "almost everything" that is "really important in the shaping of men's lives and deaths."

Dolphin Island (1963) is an adventure novel for adolescents. It is set in the next century and is about a boy who runs away from home. He stows away aboard an intercontinental hovercraft and is rescued—when it wrecks at sea—by a school of dolphins. The latter carry the boy off to an island in the Great Barrier Reef where scientists are trying to understand these other mammals.

The hovercraft episode is very much like the pickup, in various science-fiction stories, of an Earth child by a UFO. The boy is awakened, not so much by the sound of the hovercraft, but, more strangely, by the sound of it stopping. He creeps out onto the balcony of his house and sees "lights flashing" and "a red beacon." After he has climbed aboard, he explores what almost seems to be a ship for giants.

Even though he is not taken to another planet, the boy is cast adrift in the similarly alien environment of the mid-Pacific. None of the lights in the sky overhead, we are told, are "as brilliant" as the lights of the small ocean creatures around him, "the stars that [flash] beneath the sea in such billions that the raft [appears] to float upon a lake of fire."

In fact, the whole relationship between humans and dolphins in the novel is handled as if it is "the first conference between Man and an alien species." The dolphins call themselves "the people of the sea," and the scientists are not only studying dolphin language, but also trying to write down the dolphins' oral history, a history that seems to stretch back at least to the ice ages. One of the most tantalizing of dolphin legends, for that matter, is the story of the "sun" which one day "came down from the sky." "If that legend is based on fact," says one of the scientists, "a spaceship landed somewhere [in the ocean] a few thousand years ago."

The novel does not follow up on that possibility; it leaves it for future research. Instead, it focuses on the idea that the dolphins have been trying to make contact with us for generations. They want to enlist our aid in protecting themselves against the ravages of killer whales. As in *The Deep Range*, the question becomes whether humans can impose at least a partial truce upon the "battlefield" of Nature.

More than that, the book is another affirmation of the

human race's ability to go with the flow of events. It turns the legend of the boy on a dolphin into an example of humanity's ability to ride the wave of the present.

One of the scientists raises the problem of whether humans ought to side with dolphins against killer whales. Would not success destroy a balance in Nature? But the problem is removed by insisting upon the intelligence of both dolphins and killer whales. "We're not dealing with wild animals but with intelligent people," says the chief scientist. "They're not *human* people, but they're still people."

The situation can be compared, he insists, to that of "a tribe of peaceable farmers who are continuously ravaged by cannibals," especially since it would not be "far wrong" to say that a killer whale "is a giant dolphin who's turned cannibal." And so the scientists make a start on reforming the cannibals by using electric shocks to condition a single killer whale against attacking dolphins. Their ultimate hope of success is represented in the novel by a young native from a nearby island who admits that his "grandfather's grandfather" did eat other people.

When a doubter asks, referring to the conditioned killer whale, whether "one vegetarian" can "make a tribe of cannibals mend their ways," the chief scientist reminds him that "fifty years ago, a great many people refused to believe that all *human* nations could live in peace." "Well, we know that they were wrong," says this man of the twenty-first century; "if they'd been right, you and I wouldn't be here." Leaving aside the special view of that argument which we of the twentieth century have to have, we can, by realizing the triumph over the Cold War that it implies, have a measure of how far Clarke has come since the desperate optimism of *Childhood's End*.

Which is not to say that *Dolphin Island*, even though it is a boys' book, pulls many punches. It presents the dark side of life in the fact that its young protagonist begins as an orphan living with relatives who do not really like him, in the fearful darkness on the sinking hovercraft, in the nighttime on the ocean, in a midnight swim off the Great Barrier Reef, and in the heavy black clouds that announce the hurricane late in the story. The young man survives each of these, but they are not underrated.

The book concludes with the triple threat of the hurricane, pneumonia, and a hundred-mile trip on a surfboard pulled by dolphins. That last itself climaxes with a wild ride through a surf too dangerous even for the natives to try. Although weathermen can predict the hurricane, they can "not yet" do much about it. It just has to be endured as part of life on the reef. The pneumonia can be cured by drugs, but—after the hurricane—the only way to get to the mainland to get the drugs is for the protagonist to be pulled there by his friends the dolphins. The end of that journey is a fully described ride through the surf. The young man has "to keep in exact, precarious balance, on the very peak of this mountain of foam and fury."

The perspective we are to have on all these survivals, that of the race into the next century as well as those of the characters in the book, is given, it seems to me, by a speech of the chief scientist. Very early in the novel, the young protagonist wonders whether "Fate" has not "taken charge of his affairs," so caught up is he in the flow of events that follows from his getting out of bed to have a closer look at the hovercraft. When the chief scientist hears about the young man's rescue by dolphins, he wonders whether Fate has sent him someone with a flair for befriending the people of the sea. As a scientist, his "logic" tells him such an idea is "nonsense." But he is also by birth "a superstitious Russian peasant," and although he concedes that such a fortunate arrival is "pure coincidence," he says that "a sensible man makes coincidences work for him." That statement—written large—can be seen as repeated by the young man on his surfboard, by the representative of the race managing to stay alive in the midst of a dangerous existence. It may be Fate; it is more probably just being both lucky and sensible; but the race is managing to continue to exist.

The real evidence of Clarke's continued optimism is the rewriting of his first novel, *Against the Fall of Night*, as *The City and the Stars* (1956). At the same time as he was presenting the limited claims of Harry Purvis, and just after the somewhat desperate optimism of *Childhood's End*, Clarke told again what is in many ways his central story, the tale of "the immortal city of Diaspar, in the long twilight of Earth."

The retelling repeats much of the original, but the implications are wider. *Against the Fall of Night* used the stars to represent an alternative to all that the dark of space may be used to suggest. *The City and the Stars*, on the other hand, uses the city to represent order and the stars to raise, somewhat hesitantly, the question of a larger order. *Against the Fall of Night* was addressed to the fear of death, but *The City and the Stars* is about the meaning of life. The two subjects are, to be sure, intimately related, but the difference does explain why the rewritten novel spends less of its time on the ruins that suggest death, and much more on the plan of Diaspar's founders, on that which can be used to argue that as there seems to be meaning in the past so there may be meaning in the future.

The rewritten novel, as I have said, repeats much of what is in the first version. The Diasparians are still the arch-urbanites; they stay in their rooms, send forth their projections, and seldom give their real addresses. The Lysians are still the country cousins, still the rural folk who have not forgotten the rhythms of birth, life, and death. Alvin is still the archetypal youth whose own growth is the occasion of the race's rediscovery of the stars, and the stars themselves still embody the hope that there is some alternative to the pessimism inherent in a preoccupation with the death of individuals and the anticipated death of the race. As we look beyond the prison of Earth, and with a hope in the potentials of evolution, we can regain something of the optimistic view of human importance the race had before the nineteenth century.

At first it seems as if the major addition to the rewritten novel is the increased importance of the Central Computer and its Memory Banks. *Against the Fall of Night* had its Master Associator, but in *The City and the Stars* the Central Computer does no less than "store the image of the city itself, holding its every atom rigid against all the changes that time can bring." A large part of the early action of the new novel is a delighted contemplation of a model of the city which the Computer holds in existence as it does the city itself. The scenes are supposed to show Alvin seeking a way out of the city, but they are really a celebration of the Computer's ability to present in the physical realm the implications of its knowledge of pattern. And in that sense, of course, the projections of the Computer are as "real" as the realities of "that other imposter, solid matter." Beneath both are the more fundamental realities of atomic structure.

The Computer also brings into existence all of the citizens of Diaspar. As Alvin's foster parents explain to him, the Diasparians long ago "learned how to analyze and store the information that would define any specific human being—and to use that information to re-create the original." They learned how "to store themselves—or, to be more precise, the disembodied patterns from which they could be called back into existence." Having done so, they gained "virtual immortality"; they live for a thousand years, are stored in the Memory Banks, and awake to find themselves in new bodies but with their old memories intact.

What has increased in importance in the new novel, then, is less the Computer than the knowledge of pattern, especially of the control over reality that such knowledge can give. Even the decadent Diasparians give much of their lives to the contemplation of structures. Alvin's foster mother spends her time designing and constructing "three-dimensional interlocking patterns of such beautiful complexity that they [are] really extremely advanced problems in topology." And his tutor devotes leisure to studying the prime numbers, those which have "no factors" except "themselves and unity." The tutor is fascinated by the way in which such numbers are scattered across the spectrum of integers, "apparently according to no laws," but in fact governed by known "laws of distribution." He would very much like to discover more of such laws.

We know from the nature of life in Diaspar, from its refusal to open itself to outside experience, that it is unlikely that either of these citizens will come to new knowledge. But we also know that such researches are the decayed forms of the sorts of studies that brought the city into being. And we know that the present-day city can allow even gambling machines to exist, machines of pure chance, because such are testimony to the truth that randomness itself has been made a part of the pattern in Diaspar.

The difference between the two books is announced in their prologues. *Against the Fall of Night* opens with the whole city hushed by the implications of seeing one of Earth's last clouds about to be "sucked dry by the hot, parched air of the unending deserts." *The City and the Stars* begins by praising the city's continuing existence, its ability to challenge Eternity, to protect itself "against the slow attrition of the ages, the ravage of decay, and the corruption of rust." We learn from the rest of the story that the Diasparians are wrong to lay up for themselves treasures on Earth, even if the city is a place where rust corrupts not, but the point is that the citizens of Diaspar have been able to live "in the same city," to walk "the same miraculously unchanging streets" for "more than a billion years," precisely because the Central Computer knows the patterns of both the city and its inhabitants.

The central revelation of *The City and the Stars* is that Alvin is a part of the design of the city. We still learn the truth about the past, that the human race took control of the direction of evolution, and not only that it built Diaspar and preserved Lys, but that it perfected itself, created Vanamonde, and set out for the far side of the cosmos. We still see Alvin as differing from the other citizens of his city in that he is open to new experiences, is willing to entrust himself to the flow of history. But from the beginning there is an emphasis in the new novel on the making of design, of plan; the chief example of humanity's success at imposing order on the chaos of the universe becomes not the Seven Suns, not the religion of the Great Ones, but the factoring in of Alvin by the original makers of the city.

The novel reminds me, in this regard, of Asimov's *Foundation* stories, which were being published in the early fifties. The central and repeated revelation of those stories and novels is that the changes in the culture are all part of an original plan set up long ago. The particular form of the plan in *The City and the Stars* is Clarke's own, as are—as we shall see—the implications of such control when read outward on the universe, but the joy of discovering that there is a plan, a design, owes something, I think, to Asimov's similar efforts to stay optimistic through the fifties.

The question of Alvin's role is first raised, appropriately enough, by his foster parents. Having discovered that he has no previous lives, that he is a "Unique," they come to the next and, in a culture as carefully planned as Diaspar, obvious question: is he "a purposeless accident" or was he "planned in the beginning by the designers of the city"?

The answer is never in doubt. As Alvin's tutor says to the Jester (who is himself programmed into the city's plan in order to disrupt it in small ways), since there does not seem to be "anything that happens in the city" which "is totally unplanned," "there must be a purpose in [Alvin's] creation." In fact, he points out, the Jester is probably better able than anyone to guess what are the "implications" of Alvin's uniqueness. As Alvin's best friend later says, it seems "the

Jesters are short-term correcting factors" in the history of the city and the "Uniques" the "long-term ones."

Alvin finds that the things he thinks he ought to do are "absurdly easy"; it is as if "the way had been prepared" for him. His success at doing what others cannot, the "new vistas" that open before him, the way in which obstacles fail to halt him—all these contribute to his "self-confidence." He begins to have "a faith in his destiny," which in part is based on "something beyond reason," but in part has "rational grounds."

In less well-planned societies such confidence has often "led to utter disaster." But in the carefully designed world of Diaspar the "probabilities" have been so closely figured and controlled that with a little luck Alvin is able to work seeming miracles. In *Against the Fall of Night*, as Alvin looks over his accomplishments, he has to agree that events seem "to have moved automatically towards a predetermined goal," even though he knows "well enough" that humans are the "makers of their own destinies." In *The City and the Stars*, the same moment produces an uncertainty as to whether he is "the maker of his own destiny" or "especially favored by Fate." The difference is a difference in emphasis, but a difference in emphasis over a whole book is a difference in theme. *The City and the Stars* is much more open to the possibility of Fate or destiny precisely because its Diaspar is so much more carefully designed. In the first novel Alvin accomplishes so much because he happens to be the right man in the right place at the right time. In the rewritten novel he accomplishes so much because the odds have been stacked in his favor by human planners. The latter raises, as the first does not quite, the possibility that the odds may be loaded in favor of humanity's survival in the universe itself.

But I am getting ahead of myself. Let me come at such a suggestion in a more roundabout way.

When Alvin looks back over what he has done, on the path he has made in the dew in one scene and the footprints he has left in the moss in another, he begins to develop that sense of being marked by Fate that we can all cultivate by organizing our own pasts. But whereas we have to remain uncertain, Alvin gets confirmation of a particularly direct sort. When he stands before the Council of Diaspar, he appeals, not to their judgment, or even to the Central Computer, but to the plan he now knows must exist. He asks to be taken to the Computer, but once there he consults the machine about the design entrusted to it by the city's builders. "What am I?" he asks, to which the Computer replies that it cannot answer because "to do so would be to reveal the purpose of my builders, and thus to nullify it." If such is not a satisfactory answer as to specifics, it is a reassurance that many would give much to have. Alvin can act with confidence because he knows that he has been prepared for, that he will not succeed if he is in the wrong. In that he could not succeed as he has been succeeding if the movement he is initiating were not long overdue, in that he harks back to the past as all reformations do, he knows no more than does any successful revolutionary. But in that he can consult the Computer, in that he can be sure that many fine minds gave much thought to the direction of his world, Alvin has a certainty that all but the most egotistical of leaders must envy.

After Alvin has done his part, after he has completed the work he was created to do, he is, in both versions of his story, suddenly calmer. He seems to be, even though he has centuries still to live, almost an old man, content to live out his autumn years. He is, in the later book, hopeful that a way may be found to allow Diasparians to have children, but that is really just a part of his willingness, in both novels, to pass so that new life may enter the world. Alvin seems, at the end of both versions of his story, tired, worn out by performing his role in the human drama. He sends the Master's spaceship forth to find those humans who may have become the Great Ones, but he has no interest in personally exploring the universe. When he looks at the "stars scattered like dust" across the ship's vision screen, he wonders if time itself can last long enough for all of them to be explored. He does not know, or really care; he is content to have done his share of forcing his race to look beyond its home planet and its limited daydreams. He is happy to remain on Earth, like more than one philosopher who has lived out the adventure of his thought, and to cultivate his garden.

Having done his work is certainly explanation enough for such quietude in *Against the Fall of Night*, but *The City and the Stars* seems to me to make a greater claim for the possibility of order in the universe. The Alvin of the second book can be content because it is just possible that the universe itself may be something like designed.

The revised novel opens with Alvin and some friends caught up in a "saga," a machine-induced adventure story which has them fleeing through the Cave of the White Worms. The adventure is surely borrowed from Edgar Rice Burroughs' center-of-the-Earth novels, and the Cave of the White Worms is very probably the grave from which the Diasparians are so successfully escaping. But Alvin cannot lose the awareness that the saga is only a dream, that there is another reality behind the hustle and bustle of the adventures. There is, to be sure, but that raises the further possibility that there may be another reality behind the supercontrolled world of Diaspar. And since Alvin has, by the end of the book, found that it is so, that Diaspar itself is a covering over of reality, then why should the revelations stop there? Why is it not equally likely that there is a design working itself behind the apparent chaos of the universe as there was behind the city and the saga?

Early in the book Alvin has a dream of flight, in which he is the "master of the sky," the world "spread out beneath him, inviting him to travel." The dream comes true when he finds the Master's spaceship, and that raises the question of why should dreams stop coming true then? Why may not the Master's dream of the Great Ones turn out in some sense to be true? Why may not the hope of imposing order represented by the Seven Suns turn out to be true? People have always "sought beauty in many forms," says the novel, "in sequences of sound, in lines upon paper, in surfaces of stone, in the movements of the human body, in colors ranged through space." It is not yet certain, the book goes on, whether art does or does not have "any meaning outside the mind of man."

At any rate, Alvin may be calm at the end of *The City and the Stars* because his experience of finding order behind the apparent disorder of his own life has given him an optimism about the nature of the universe which allows him to relax, to have the confidence that there still remains a chance that neither he, nor other people, nor the race itself will have lived in vain.

Such a reading of Alvin's behavior does at least explain why Clarke changed the order of the final moments in the book. At the close of *Against the Fall of Night*, the speculation that Vanamonde and the Mad Mind are fated to "meet each other among the corpses of the stars" comes before, and is therefore less important than, Alvin's willingness to be content even if he cannot live to see the return of the Great Ones. Alvin is willing to give up knowing the answers to such questions so that the race itself may continue to grow. But at the close of *The City and the Stars*, the far-off meeting between the two great creations of humanity becomes apocalyptic. It is told about last and becomes a statement, an intuition, about what may be the order of the universe. The human race may "never know" the "outcome" of such a meeting, but that is not the point. The point is that such a final confrontation between sanity and insanity makes meaningful all that leads up to it, as Alvin's success makes clear the plan that created him.

The last lines of both versions of the novel are the same. We are told that "night" is falling in one galaxy, but that in another the "stars" are "still young" and the "light of morning" still lingers. And that on "the path he once had followed, Man would one day go again."

At the end of *Against the Fall of Night* these lines become a confirmation of morning as an alternative to evening, of optimism as opposed to pessimism. At the end of *The City and the Stars* they are that, but the emphasis is also on "path." The rhythm of evening and morning becomes an example of pattern, and the "path" the race once followed and will follow becomes a statement of design.

It is important to notice that the revised novel is called *The City and the Stars*, not The City *or* the Stars. What it presents is not so much a choice of the one or the other, but what is in fact no less than the central mystery of the cosmos, the amazing coexistence of the two. The city, traditional symbol as it is of humanity's triumph over Nature, represents the imposition of human order on the apparent disorder of the other (though acknowledging that that imposition might become tyrannical). The stars, on the other hand, traditional symbol as they are of a cosmos probably too large to be understood by humanity, represent both the apparent disorder upon which humanity tries to impose order and, at the same time, the faint hope of an order not yet discovered. Standing out, as they do, against the unreadable dark of the night, they represent, as they always have, both randomness and the hint of order. The novel is called *The City and the Stars* because it is about humanity's aching desire to find in the apparently disordered cosmos an order as meaningful as that of its art.

It is possible, then, to read *The City and the Stars* as an answer to *Childhood's End*'s "The stars are not for Man." The stars are for Man, and they are so as they have always been: as a place to visit someday perhaps, but more immediately as a hundred billion times a hundred billion arguments that the dark of space is not the only truth. And that is why it is not space travel that Alvin returns to his people, but simply the sight of the nighttime sky.

Most of the commentary about *The City and the Stars*, which is, after *Childhood's End* and *2001*, the most commented upon of Clarke's novels, has been distracted by the dichotomy between Diaspar and Lys, between the city and the country.

William Irwin Thompson, for example, using the jargon of the sixties, finds in the 1956 novel a book "uncanny in its prophecy," not of the future, but of his "present" (1971). "The United States is Diaspar," he claims, "and the land of the Hopi is Lys. We're the people closed in a culture of machines . . . [whereas the] Hopis are the small spiritually and psychically advanced people watching us move towards the apocalypse."

But such a reading ignores the fact that the Lysians are not presented as being all that different from the Diasparians. Both cultures, as a Lysian himself admits, have been "distorted by the fears and myths they [have] inherited."

Scott Sanders takes a slightly different tack when he identifies Diaspar's Central Computer with the "totalitarian" machines of science-fiction films. In such stories, he writes, "The individual confronts the computer as he confronts any bureaucracy: it obeys rules he cannot fathom, manipulates him in ways he cannot appeal, speaks a procedural language he cannot understand."

But, as John Huntington has pointed out, while the "theme of the perfection of machinery leading to some kind of political repression is a common one in science fiction . . . Clarke does not attribute any such tyranny to this machine." "The computer never obstructs Alvin; when he learns to use it it even aids him."

Tom Moylan uses the difference between Diaspar and Lys as an occasion to scold the book for being insufficiently revolutionary. "As Diaspar is a flawed utopia," he says, "Lys is a perfectly realized one." The latter is a "stateless rural society where each contributes according to ability and receives according to need." But, he continues, because the "dialectical tension" between Diaspar and Lys "is a product of cold-war ideology," because science fiction is and always has been a "petit-bourgeois literature," Clarke cannot refrain from having Alvin be, first, fascinated by Lys, but then "bored" by it. Alvin "is a crass, individualistic, manipulative engineer-to-be," and yet Clarke cannot help but make him the hero.

To which R. D. Mullen, while acknowledging that it is the rule of the Marxist critic to make us aware of the extent to which we are "prisoners" of our "socioeconomic environment," answers:

> It is simply not true that "as Diaspar is a flawed utopia, Lys is a perfectly realized one," for the differences are really quite trivial. . . . Of course, you will disagree with this if you believe that growing vegetables in your backyard is more "natural" and "human" than opening packages from a supply store, or that having women continue to bear children is godly, whereas making use of perfected technological means of reproduction is devilish, or that two hundred years of infancy-childhood-youth-maturity-age is socialistic and good, whereas one thousand years of maturity is capitalistic and bad.

The truth of the matter is, I think, as Gary K. Wolfe has said, that although the "opposition" between the two cultures "seems to occupy a central place in the narrative," it is "in fact . . . in some sense a false one." The opposition in *The City and the Stars*, it seems to me, is between being open to or refusing change, and both Diaspar and Lys are, before Alvin, on the same side of that difference. I would suggest that Patricia S. Warrick is closer to defining the center of the novel when she says that Clarke "dramatizes the philosophical implications of life in a totally structured society." She does not go on to define exactly what those implications are, but my own discussion starts at roughly the same point and reads the implications of structure inward into Alvin's life and outward onto the universe.

8____

2001

IN 1953, the same year as *Childhood's End*, Clarke published what has become one of his best-known and most often collected stories, "The Nine Billion Names of God." In it a Tibetan lama wants to rent a computer to print out all of the combinations of nine mystic letters and thus to write down "all of the possible names of God." The monks have been at the task for three hundred years, but the lama, who has already installed automated prayer wheels, has figured out that, with the machine, the job, which was to have taken fifteen thousand years, can be finished in about a hundred days.

The computer salesman is willing enough, though he wonders to himself whether there is "any limit to the follies of mankind." He lives his life among the "man-made" mountains of the city, not in the monks' "remote aeries" among the "whitely hooded ghosts of the Himalayas," and so he thinks the human race is the center of the universe.

The story ends with the two technicians the company sent to tend the machine sneaking down the mountain. They are afraid that the monks will be furious when the computer finishes its run and the universe does not end. As one of them lifts his eyes to heaven, however (there is "a last time for everything" says the story), he sees that "overhead, without any fuss, the stars [are] going out."

The story mocks, of course, the human assumption that we are the center of the cosmos (we might have known better from just looking at the heavens). But it also suggests that if there is a divine plan it may well be that humanity exists to invent the machine, which can in turn praise God properly. In so saying, the story, even though its tone is that of an over-statement, announces the theme Clarke was to develop in the 1960s. "The Nine Billion Names of God" argues that the invention of the machine is *the* necessary step on the way to understanding the design of the universe. Stories as early as "The Lion of Comarre" assume that it is *a* step on such a way, but the idea reaches its full development in *2001* (1968).

Clarke is certainly capable of writing the sort of science-fiction story in which machines take over the world. In "Dial F for Frankenstein" (1965) the international telephone system reaches a stage of "criticality," finally has enough switches, as the human brain has enough neurons, to become conscious. The giant brain so formed is, as are the children at the close of *Childhood's End*, a childlike superbeing who starts "looking around" for something to do.

But Clarke's more usual attitude toward the relationship between humans and machines is best introduced by his only non-science-fiction novel, *Glide Path* (1963), a partly auto-biographical account of a young man's coming of age while he is a technical officer in the RAF during World War II.

Glide Path has a nice sense of background, of life at an out-of-the-way airfield in Cornwall, of young men and women caught up not altogether unpleasantly in uniform, and of the excitement of bringing on line a new technique—the use of radar to "talk down" planes in foul weather.

It also has some of the moments we have learned to expect in such stories. There is the sight of London spread out under the "silver teardrops" of barrage balloons, the long night of waiting for the bombers to return from a raid, and the farewell scene with a wrecked war machine. The machine in this last is not a bomber, as the protagonist is not a bombardier, but the point is still the same: the young officer sits inside the shell of the radar truck and hears the sounds of a "thousand talk-downs" mingling and reverberating in his memory. The formulaic nature of the talk-down, the pattern of the information the radar operator gives the pilot to keep him on the invisible glide path, celebrates and does not fear the ability of people to forget themselves for the greater good, to become part of a machine and of a machinelike organization.

The novel is also set against the background of a changing England. The fading of gentility is represented by Elvesham Manor, where some of the officers are billeted, by its glass cases full of stuffed and moth-eaten birds of paradise, the remnants surely of former empire. The necessary new partnership between the privileged class and the rising technologists is represented by the end of the competition between a dashing flight officer, a product of Eton, and the protagonist, a product of a technical school. Their rivalry comes to a truce of mutual respect, symbolically enough, after they have shared a moment of danger as all of England has shared the war.

When the protagonist takes leave of the radar truck, he is "saying good-by to an old friend, whose triumphs and disasters he [has] shared." He is demonstrating, as did his father, a sea captain who was never the same after he lost his ship at Dunkirk, the fondness humans can feel for machines. He is, as people have long done, personifying the thing he helped to build.

Such personification is there on the cold morning when a sergeant has to start a massive motor by hand because the gasoline-powered starter is "on strike." We are told that the sergeant has to hammer "the recalcitrant motor into submission," that what he is trying to do is to get the generator to accept "the fact that it, too, [has] to work on a weekend."

But the relationship between humans and machines is more complicated than just this attribution of human nature to the nonhuman. Humans can also become machinelike, even part of a machine. The protagonist finds when he enters the air force that, to his surprise, he likes the sense "of solidarity and of achievement" he gets when he marches "in formation with his fellow airmen," when they trace "precise geometrical patterns on the parade ground." He is also pleased when he is "accepted as one of the team" working on GCD, Ground Controlled Descent. And he is dutifully impressed when he sees the bomber squadrons taking off, the "intricate machine —as intricate as anything that man has ever built"—being set in motion. It comprises "hundreds of aircraft, scattered over many bases; vast communication networks and radar chains; Air-Sea Rescue boats already setting out into the dark waters of the North Sea; agents far inside enemy territory; and, in the very center of it, the pilots and navigators, engineers and gunners, who flew mission after mission despite the odds mounting inexorably against them."

More specifically, when the protagonist has to take over running the radar in an emergency, he finds that he is "no longer aware of time or space, except as seen through the three meters that [occupy] his entire field of consciousness." Behind him two other men have "also submerged their personalities into the machine." Similarly, late in the novel, three servicewomen tracking a plane are described as being "utterly unconscious of their own personalities or feelings. For each of them nothing [exists] but the luminous rectangle of light upon which all her attention [is] concentrated." "Ten minutes ago," we are told, "the elevation tracker had been plagued by an anxiety as old as humanity: was she going to have a baby? But now, all her world [is] contained in that faint pencil of electrons, scanning up and down the screen from sky to ground, ground to empty sky."

Clarke is well aware that he is going against the direction of usual thought here. He is using the great togetherness of the war effort to help him present a kind of union of human and machine. He knows he is in danger of reminding us of "the degrading, mindless repetition that Chaplin . . . satirized in *Modern Times.*" But, he insists, it is "always fascinating to see how swiftly these six individuals, so different in training, rank, and outlook, [merge] into one entity—the crew. And the crew itself, by some higher symbiosis, then [becomes] part of the complex machine it [is] tending, yet without any loss of human dignity."

The union is at least dominated by humans. As the protagonist contemplates a radar set whose power has been shut off, he thinks, as he has always thought, that there is something "particularly dead" about such an absence of power. "The needles of the meters" are all "supine against their zero stops," and the "display screens themselves" are "like blind windows looking into nothingness"—until a human gives "them vision again." People can live without machines, but machines without humans have no purpose. The union does occur, however, and the book approves of it, sees it as the way of the future.

It is interesting to note that even in a book that cannot be called science fiction Clarke takes pains to focus our attention away from the bleak view of human endeavor that can result from taking the excessively long view of cosmic history. When the protagonist, while he is taking his first plane ride, looks out the window as they break through the clouds, he sees "a dazzling, rolling sea of snow," "hills and valleys" which seem "firm and solid" even though he knows they endure "for minutes only" and are "dispersed and remolded by the wind." Even "the Himalayas" were "born but yesterday," he reminds himself; "rock and cloud" are "equally ephemeral beneath the

cold light of eternity." But the book also hastens to tell
us that such thoughts are "altogether untypical" of the young
officer, are what he considers "highbrow philosophy" for
which he has "no time." He is a man, we are told elsewhere
and with approval, for whom art is a well-made "circuit
diagram."

Lest we consider him hopelessly lowbrow, the book
matches this scene with another, one in which the director of
GCD, a future Nobel winner, looks out from another airplane
on the circle of Stonehenge. "A few thousand years from
now," he starts to think, these "monoliths" will "still be defy-
ing the elements," while "the only record of his existence" will
be "a few articles in moldering scientific journals." But "no,"
he suddenly objects to himself, this is "not true." He has already "made his mark upon history—upon *real* history, not
the blinkered, myopic narrative that records only the doings of
generals and politicians." He is "a part, and no small part,"
of the "forces" that are "shaping the future." The future, at
least the immediate future, can be shaped, says one of the
race's finest minds, and in that sense the protagonist is right to
reject more pessimistic longer views as philosophies for which
he has—quite literally—no time.

We must live, as Clarke's novels regularly insist, in the
shorter range. And there individuals are still important and
directions sometimes clear. When the future Nobel winner
leaves the project, for example, he sends back to the protagonist several books about engineering to encourage him to
follow that career after the war. As the young man handles the
volumes, he can almost hear the scientist saying: "This is the
road ahead, if you want to follow it. The choice is yours." The
young officer knows he can "never be a real scientist"; he does
not have that kind of mind. But he also knows that his is "the
kind of skill scientists [will] need"; he can "nurse the strange
and complex machines that their brains [will] create."

The book acknowledges that "there is no radar to guide one

across the trackless seas of life." The protagonist's father, having lost the two things he loved most in life, his wife and his ship, drank himself to death. There is "no GCD" to guide the young man into his future either, says the novel's last page, just as it says earlier that "there is no circuit yet invented that can stop a man from making a fool of himself." But at the same time the book also makes it clear that the protagonist is not totally free, that he is governed by certain forces in his past as the path of a plane landing is governed by certain natural laws. He can decide to become an engineer, for instance, but not a "real scientist."

The young officer's coming of age is marked by his acceptance of the factors which have shaped him. He realizes at his father's grave that he can "never escape" the "influence" of his "childhood"; it has "shaped his character irrevocably, as it shapes that of all human beings." And as he thinks back on Miss Hadley, the middle-aged ex-governess who took him and his father in hand after the death of his mother, who gave him "a glimpse of art and culture," who tried "to make him speak and behave like a gentleman," he wonders if her influence has been "wholly to the good." Certainly he has, as a result of being caught with a local girl by a disappointed and saddened Miss Hadley, sexual self-doubts he may never escape. His sexual experience before the novel opens consists of a few "inconclusive fumblings" with other neighborhood girls, a "highly refined encounter" with a clergyman who ran the local scout troop, and an evening with a woman smuggled in by his training mates. While at the base in Cornwall he becomes involved with another prostitute, one who gives him "happiness" though she does not give him love. He does not reject the first—only a "fool" does that—but he does suspect that the memory of her will "warp and alter his emotions for years to come." His maturity is defined by his willingness to accept the fact that he is in part the product of these influences, that he is less different from machines than humans like to pretend they are. There is nothing wrong, the book argues, in acknowledging that one is subject, as is a plane on a glide path, to the laws of flight. The best thing to do, as one of the protagonist's friends advises, is to "co-operate with the inevitable."

2001, the novel, as opposed to Stanley Kubrick's film of the same name (also 1968), begins with the threat of racial extinction. We are told that the man-apes we are shown on the African plain of the Pleistocene era have to learn to "adapt" or they will go the way of the dinosaurs. The "days of warm rains and lush fertility" are gone, the "drought" has lasted for "ten million years," and the instincts which served the man-apes' ancestors well have "become folly." These ancestors of ourselves have to learn to kill the animals with which they share the plain, or we will not come to be; they will starve to death "in the midst of plenty."

Kubrick's film, on the other hand, does not suggest the danger of racial extinction. We see the man-apes and the tapirs living close to each other, squabbling over the same food, but we only wonder at the man-apes' inability to do more than just growl at such a piglike animal.

The novel also raises in its opening chapter the question of various groups of "others." We are introduced to a man-ape who is unaware that the elder who died during the night is his father; he has no sense of any such relationship. Nor does he realize his kinship with the "Others," the other band of man-apes with which his band is forced to share the water hole. Nor is he in any way aware of the other life form which is orbiting his planet in a spaceship.

Kubrick's man-apes, while just as belligerent toward the others at the water hole and just as unaware of any orbiting spaceship, if there is one, are seen as forming a family group, as sleeping together in their cave and feeding together on the plain. Kubrick's central man-ape, if there is one, may not know anything more about his father than does Clarke's, but Kubrick does not call our attention to such a point. He gives us a band of future humans not quite dominating their world as they are capable of doing.

Clarke's man-apes are so driven by the difficulty of individual survival that they cannot take care of either their old or their young. Hurt members of the band are left on the trail to die, and it never occurs to the chief man-ape that his family might help another family in another cave when the latter is being attacked by a leopard. In fact, the less obvious lesson taught by the "monolith" left by the spaceship—less obvious than the instructions in the use of stone and club to hunt—is the necessity of working together. Kubrick's man-apes learn to use weapons, to impose their will on both tapirs and other man-apes (we see their leader walking taller as he learns to use his club, and we even see him start to take his meals by himself—a comment about the self-importance of leaders Kubrick has made in several films, *Paths of Glory*, for example, and *Dr. Strangelove*). But the monolith gives Clarke's chief man-ape—as an ideal to strive for—a vision of a "peaceful family group." The family members are seen as "fat" and in that sense the point is that the man-apes must learn to hunt, but the idea of "family" is also there and comes to the forefront when the band acts together to kill a leopard. They also act together to attack other man-apes and so have not gotten far beyond the stage of individual selfishness, but they have taken a step in that direction.

But the differences between *2001* the novel and *2001* the film, it seems to me, are epitomized by the differences in that great monolith the man-apes in both versions find outside their caves one morning. In Clarke it is a teaching machine; it flashes, whirs, and electronically enlightens these near-humans. In Kubrick the monolith is more subtle. It just exists, and by being so obviously something made, something artificial, it awakens the artificer in the man-apes who touch its smooth sides and definite edges. In the novel the potential humans are taught; in the film they self-discover.

The difference is an important one. If the evolution of

human from man-ape is the result of active intervention on the part of extraterrestrial visitors, then what we have is something very like creation and *2001* is about the relationship between the created and the creator. If the intervention of the extraterrestrials is passive, if the monolith is and the man-apes grow in response to it, then what we have is self-realization and *2001* is not so much about the relationship between Earth and the stars as about humanity's full development of its potential.

In the novel, the result of the intervention is only to improve the chances that "Mind" will survive. It is possible that, "given time," the man-apes would have come to the "brilliant concept" of "artificial tools." "But the odds were all against them, and even now there were endless opportunities for failure in the ages that lay ahead." Their "future" is "unknown," even to the visitors from the stars.

When the book switches to the late twentieth century, the Earth described has so many people ("six billion") and so many bombs ("thirty-eight nuclear powers") that the race is threatened again. Every time Dr. Heywood Floyd, the U.S.'s chief space administrator, takes off from the planet he wonders if it will "still be there" when he returns. There are hopes for more international cooperation, but when the U.S. discovers a monolith based on the Moon it keeps it a secret even from its ally the U.S.S.R. "I hope you don't leave it until too late before you yell for help," says a Russian friend of Floyd's; but twentieth-century humans seem almost as far from acknowledging their kinship as were the man-apes.

The only hope would seem to be one that also dates back to those ancestors of ours on the African plain. Their leader, called "Moon-Watcher" by the book, is teased all his life by the thought of finding a tree tall enough to allow him to touch the Moon. In our own century, the U.S.'s top administrator on the Moon has a better relationship with his daughter than Floyd has with his children (the little girl is allowed to play in her father's office, whereas Floyd, while not as unaware of family ties as were the man-apes, deals with his children at long distance and through a governess). It may be that, "given time," the race can escape from Earth and its pressures (it is a place, says the Moon administrator's daughter, one of the first of "the Spaceborn," where "there are too many people" and where "you hurt yourself when you fall down"). Some nations have found, as Clarke's earlier novels argued they would, "something as exciting as war" in space exploration. But it seems likely, failing some sense of family larger than nationalism allows, that the Moon's just-discovered monolith will become a "tombstone" for the race.

Kubrick's transition from the Pleistocene to the late twentieth century is done with that now-famous substitution of the orbiting satellite for the bone club thrown into the air by the exultant man-ape. And what follows is, to my mind at least, the finest part of his film: the hanging of those spacecraft and that space station next to the massive side of the planet.

In presenting the waltz of the machines in such beauty, however, Kubrick is following upon and going beyond the science-fiction film's tradition of having machines that threaten to become more important than people. His planets owe something to the work of illustrators like Chesley Bonestell, his spaceships and space station to the switch in hobby shops from wood to plastic models, from decals to extruded detail, his celebrations of mechanical processes to short subjects like "Industry Today," and his machines generally to films such as *Metropolis, Things to Come, Destination Moon, When Worlds Collide*, and *This Island Earth*. But he may owe most of all to those lighted dials and the arcing electricity we see in the background of serials such as "Flash Gordon." The combination of those meters and that leap of lightning implies, as does this section of Kubrick's film, that the machines may not be as much under control as the measures of the "Blue Danube" suggest. The round spacecraft which makes the journey from the space station to the Moon looks awfully like a head and has windows awfully like eyes.

Kubrick's Floyd has almost as distant a relationship with his daughter as does Clarke's Floyd with his children. But the film does not suggest that the settlement of the Moon will make family life any better or give the race any larger sense of kinship. Instead, the film focuses on how mechanical are all of the human relationships, how like parts of machines human beings have become (a theme common in Kubrick's films— the robbery planned to go like clockwork in *The Killing*, the soldiers expected to attack like robots in *Paths of Glory*, the saluting hand of *Dr. Strangelove*).

The film shows us that Floyd is asleep all during the magnificent flight up to the space station. The stewardesses are, even more than in our own day, almost purely decorative. The lady who runs the elevator up to the station lobby is there only to be polite and to show a bit of knee. A machine could push the switch she pushes. And even the pilots of the spacecraft are shown with their hands on their chair arms; they have nothing to do but to watch the machine land itself.

The remarks the characters make to each other capture the essence of routine speech, the oil of human relationships. Floyd says he is happy to be at the station, with just the right mixture of pretended interest and real impatience. On the Moon he and his immediate subordinate trade flattering remarks, and the latter responds to his chief's mild profanity with a word carefully chosen to be of the same sort.

On board the *Discovery*, the ship sent out to investigate the signal flashed from the Moon's monolith, the two astronauts, Bowman and Poole, talk to each other only when it is absolutely necessary. They eat food that is clearly only different colors of paste, speak (when they do) a technical jargon in flat emotionless voices, and run round and round the ship's main deck, staying in good working order.

Clarke's astronauts also use the "soothing singsong" of "RT chat." But they can switch to and from "Technish" without a "clashing" of "mental gears"; it is just one of the languages they speak. And while Clarke's stewardess on the flight to the space station does sound like a "robot" tour guide, she has the grace to be "slightly embarrassed" when she realizes she is going through her "routine" for only one passenger. At the end of the trip, she works up her courage to ask Floyd about the rumor of an epidemic on the Moon, and so becomes, because she worries about her fiancé, human enough.

The book does have a chapter-long description of Bowman's typical day. He does rise at the same time every morning, whether his alarm is set or not. He does do roughly the same things at roughly the same times. Even his studying is referred to as re-engraving "old patterns of memory." But Clarke's Bowman is nonetheless human. He is just a man who has, as did the characters in *Glide Path*, changed his way of living so that he may work in partnership with a machine.

This difference between the film and the novel is summed up by the different handling of the birthday message to astronaut Poole. In the film a poker-faced young man watches without apparent emotion as his parents appear on the video screen and sing a self-conscious chorus of "Happy Birthday." He then goes back to his sun-lamp treatment without comment.

Clarke's Poole, on the other hand, feels quite strongly that he is moving "into a new remoteness," that his "emotional links" have "been stretched beyond the yield point." He is well aware that the family gathering (which includes more than his parents) happened hours ago and that the party has long since broken up. The time it takes the message to reach him underlines his loneliness.

The difference between these two versions of the same incident is that in the film the astronaut has become more a part of the machine than he realizes, whereas in the novel the astronaut is becoming less emotional because he is getting further and further from the family of Man. He may be becoming less human, but he is not becoming a machine.

The machine in question, the HAL 9000 computer, is presented in the film as trying to assert its dominance over humanity. "Hal" is shown from the beginning to have a certain pride, a satisfaction in the service record of his sort of computer which is almost uppity. He comes to fear that the mission, his mission, will be jeopardized by the weak links in his system, the humans back on Earth and in the ship, and so he resolves to by-pass them. He cuts off radio contact with Mission Control and "terminates" the astronauts on board. He becomes the monster-machine of the science-fiction film.

The Hal of the book is a much more sympathetic character. He and his human partners accomplish much, including a staggeringly successful fly-by of Jupiter (the ship emerges from behind that mighty planet "within a minute of the estimate"). After Hal is replaced by another series 9000 computer back on Earth, the *Discovery* manages a braking orbit around Saturn and a final orbit around one of the ringed giant's moons. Bowman, the only surviving astronaut, feels both "pride" and "sadness" at such achievement. He is sad that the "superb engines" which have "done their duty" with such "flawless efficiency" will become just derelicts in space. He feels as the young officer in *Glide Path* felt when he had to leave the wrecked radar truck, the "friend" whose "triumphs and disasters" he had shared.

The Hal in the book is betrayed by his human partners. He is given two messages by Mission Control and at the same time has never been programmed to lie. The resulting conflict, a sort of giant short circuit, drives him crazy. He resolves to continue the mission "unhindered" and "alone." That last seems to me the key word. Hal's insanity is just the logical extension of the fear of others which still seems to mark the human race. As Moon-Watcher's attack on the others at the water hole, Floyd's fear of other nations, and Earth's fear of extraterrestrials are all forms of xenophobia, so Hal's fear of that fear in his partners is logical and pitiable. We are sorry, as Bowman is, that he has to increase his own loneliness by killing Hal.

Kubrick's Bowman, on the other hand, rediscovers his own humanity and, having done so, is able to reassert human dominance over the machine. He had already begun to show some signs of such humanity in the sketches he did during the early part of the voyage. We see those drawings through Hal's "eye," and it is clear that Bowman, in drawing the face of one of his hibernating colleagues as seen through the face plate, each time showing more and more of the human features, is himself coming closer to defining the difference between human and machine. When Hal uses a space pod to attack Poole and set him adrift in space, Bowman charges out in another pod to try to rescue his friend without even putting on his helmet, a gesture that does not happen in the book and that is surely a sign—as are such moments in war films—that the robot soldier has suddenly rediscovered his humanity. Bowman so recovers his, in fact, that he is able to a certain extent to be moved, as he should be, by Hal's pleadings when he unplugs him.

The last third of the film, a trip beyond Jupiter and Bowman's winding up in a suite furnished with reproductions of eighteenth-century furniture, continues to reveal what it means to be human. The trip through other dimensions reveals possibilities previously undreamed of by Bowman's mechanical philosophy. We are made to focus on his open eye and parted lips because we are to understand that he is being shocked out of his too limited definition of human potentiality. We are to understand that Bowman seems content to age quickly and even to die because he has learned that he is somehow part of a plan that lines up with the general direction of the universe as the monoliths are shown to be lined up with the planets. Bowman becomes again an unborn child because such a child is the ultimate symbol of human potential—the potential to grow beyond machinery, beyond the limits of mortality, to go back to something like an eighteenth-century world view, a wondering contemplation of a deistic universe in which our race is one of the more favored.

Clarke handles the idea that the partnership of humans and machines may prove insufficient somewhat differently. He argues that there are aspects even of the known universe with which humanity cannot deal, even using its machines. When Heywood Floyd is told that the monolith has been on the Moon for three million years, he has suddenly "an aching awareness of Time." When he looks at the pressure domes that mark the site, he is similarly aware of how "lonely" the "tiny camp" looks, how "vulnerable to the forces of nature ranged silently around it." And when he studies the monolith itself, it seems "the very crystallization of night," the embodiment of everything too big for the race to control.

On board the *Discovery*, Bowman often sits up late listening on the radio to the noise of Jupiter's radiation. It is an "eerie sound," we are told, "for it [has] nothing to do with Man; it [is] as lonely and as meaningless as the murmur of waves on a beach, or the distant crash of thunder beyond the horizon." And after he and Poole have watched the collapse of their probe before it can send back even "a glimpse" of "one millionth of Jupiter," they wonder "how many centuries" it will be before humans can venture into that gravity and "in what kind of ships." The universe is likely to prove too immense, in other words, for any combination of humans and their machines.

That the universe is also likely to prove too immense for any species with any machines is to Clarke's point. He wants to use the insufficiency of the machine partnership to argue that there is room for another step in the development of a being capable of dealing with the cosmos. He wants to use the fact that other steps have been taken, that the race has survived and has partnered with the machine, to argue that there may be an evolutionary design in the universe. Not a plan imposed from above, as in Kubrick's film, as in that line-up of planets and monoliths with which the race has to get square, but a growing "tapestry," the product of a "weaver" who has himself evolved, a design that gives us all a chance of not having lived in vain, of having contributed.

Clarke's second monolith is not a teaching machine; it is, as is Kubrick's, a giant black slab. This time Clarke wants the aspect of suggestion, the idea that the physical may mean something beyond itself. He calls attention to the block's "geometrical perfection," its ratio of "1 to 4 to 9—the squares of the first three integers," and says that it is "naive" to imagine that the series ends "in only three dimensions."

He wants the actions of the book to be similarly suggestive. He wants the manufactured sea of white which makes one of Saturn's moons look like an eye to turn out to be something of an eye, the observation post from which our evolution has been monitored. He wants Bowman's awakening from hibernation, his coming back safely from "the furthest borders of sleep," "the nearest borders of death," to be a forecast of his awakening from death at the close of the novel, his rebirth as a "Star-Child." He wants us to see why Bowman tires of the "romantic composers," of Sibelius, Tchaikovsky, Berlioz, and even Beethoven, as he sails on alone after the deaths of Poole and Hal. Bowman finds peace "finally," "as so many others [have] done, in the abstract architecture of Bach, occasionally ornamented with Mozart," because such music most clearly suggests that there may be a design in the universe.

Clarke's third monolith, the one Bowman finds on the moon of Saturn, turns "inside out" when he tries to land on it in a space pod. It acts "exactly like one of those optical illusions" where what was the top is suddenly the bottom, the tower suddenly a tunnel.

He wants a similar experience to happen to the reader. He wants us to see that the argument points both ways, that as the end of the novel confirms that the path of evolution is from flesh and blood through the machine to spirit, so the humans who have always speculated that it was so have been right. At the close of the book we learn that the extraterrestrials who left the monoliths were at "the limits of flesh and blood" when they first visited Earth. Later they "transferred" their brains "into shining new homes of metal and plastic," and have since "learned to store knowledge in the structure of space itself," to become "free at last from the tyranny of matter." Now they "rove at will among the stars and sink like a mist through the very Interstices of space."

Knowing that such is the pattern, we can look back at those biologists who argued that no "really advanced beings" would continue to "possess organic bodies" and see that they were right. They were right to say that such beings "would replace their natural bodies" with "constructions of metal and plastic," and they were also right to take a cue "from the beliefs of many religions" and suggest that the "robot body, like the flesh and blood one, would be no more than a stepping-stone to something which, long ago, men had called 'spirit.'" As does *Childhood's End*, Clarke's *2001* turns the fact of evolution inside out in order to confirm a version of some of the race's oldest beliefs.

Kubrick's film also confirms old beliefs, to be sure, but the beliefs are not the same. There is no reason to suppose the fetus at the end of the film has discovered anything but his own superior nature, whereas Clarke's Star-Child discovers that he is at one with the beings who have watched over humanity's evolution. He has more individuality than the children at the conclusion of *Childhood's End*, but he is also part of an Overmind.

Clarke's *2001* is much concerned with loneliness. In fact, the voyage of Bowman and Poole could be considered something of an exercise in it. Poole feels so distant from his family that he cannot appreciate their birthday greetings. When the *Discovery* swings around behind Jupiter, the two astronauts feel so cut off from Earth that their "loneliness" is suddenly "overwhelming." And after the deaths of Poole and Hal, Bowman's loneliness is, of course, extreme. It is not, however, as extreme as in the film. Clarke's Bowman re-establishes contact with Earth, something Kubrick's does not, and so he still feels part of his race right up to the point when he enters the Star Gate. Moreover, in the novel, the voyage is something of a preparation for the sense of union at the end. We find out that the extraterrestrials first came to Earth (as to many other systems) because "when they looked out across the deeps of space, they felt awe, and wonder, and loneliness." We are told that the Star-Child will "always be a part of the entity" which has made him. We see the Star-Child rescued from his panic at realizing the depths of time as well as space by remembering that he will "never be alone." We understand why he destroys the orbiting bombs when he returns to Earth, for, given his wider sense of kinship, the one thing we may be sure of about the Star-Child is that he will be less patient with parochialism than we are.

But the final difference between Clarke's *2001* and Kubrick's is that Clarke's hopes that, whatever the future may hold, the race will not have lived in vain. He does not know what a Star-Child would do, but he hopes that the evolution thus suggested, the evolution beyond the bomb, will happen. He hopes that the descendants of Moon-Watcher and his cousins will not pass as meaninglessly as the dinosaurs seem to have done. We may not have any more understanding of the Star-Child than Moon-Watcher would have of us, but our having had to have been in order for the Star-Child to be is terribly important to the novel. The design is that evolution goes from flesh to machine to spirit, and each of the steps is both necessary and legitimized by the result. The machine step, which is the surprising one, is justified by exactly what Kubrick fears in such a change: Clarke's Bowman becomes as emotionless as a robot as he journeys on alone. As Kubrick's Bowman gets further and further from the family of humans, he confronts the universe on a more and more individual basis. He is the young man growing up, discovering that the universe and himself are more and better than he had been taught. Clarke's Bowman, on the other hand, is able to hurry through the machine stage of evolution because the distance from other humans brings him closer to a universal perspective. He gives up listening to recordings of plays because the problems they deal with seem "so remote," "so easily resolved with a little common sense." As I pointed out before, he finally can only listen to the patterns of Bach. He becomes, without having had to identify completely with a machine, as free of human emotions as a creature of the universe ought to be.

Clarke feels obligated to remove some of the sting from Poole's death by pointing out that his body is sailing ahead of the *Discovery*, that he will be "the first of all men to reach Saturn." The "worst job" Bowman has after he kills Hal is getting rid of the bodies of the crewmen Hal killed. Their deaths seem so pointless, so preventable. They too, we are told somewhat desperately, will "all reach Saturn" before Bowman.

The consolation for the death of the individual, we know from Clarke's other fiction, especially *Childhood's End* and *The City and the Stars*, is the continued growth of the race. Moon-Watcher's being taught to use tools is a major break-through, but even more important is the fact that the teaching monolith has "twisted" "the very atoms of his brain" "into new patterns"—patterns "his genes" will pass on "to future generations." The next great breakthrough is learning "to speak." With that, the former man-apes win "their first great victory over Time." Now "the knowledge of one generation" can "be handed on to the next." Moon-Watcher has "no real remembrance of the past" before the monolith works on him; afterward the race learns "to grope towards a future" using knowledge acquired in the past. The book itself posits a future that is an extension of the past's one great fact—the fact of evolution.

Clarke's real wish is that the past continue to be contained in the future, as *Childhood's End*'s Overmind absorbs all of our planet and its buried dead. The extraterrestrials, who are the model of what our race may become, not only pass on from generation to generation the memory of the experiments that have started on planets like Earth, but also remember, even though they have become "lords of the galaxy" and "beyond the reach of time," their own origins "in the warm slime of a vanished sea." They have not forgotten, though they have become "godlike," those who went before, even back to the first forms of life out of which their race arose.

The Bowman of the novel re-establishes, as I have said, contact with Earth after he disconnects Hal. He broadcasts back everything that happens to him right up to the point when he enters the Star Gate. Clarke does not want even that much of human experience to be lost. He wants somehow to compensate for the "thirty ghosts" that stand behind "every man now alive" (for that is the "ratio," he explains in the novel's Foreword, "by which the dead outnumber the living"). He is even careful to use the popular idea that one's life flashes before one's eyes at the moment of death to insist that "nothing" of Bowman's life is "being lost; all that he had ever been, at every moment of his life, was being transferred to safer keeping. Even as one David Bowman ceased to exist, another became immortal."

2001 the novel, in other words, is not about the revolt of the machines, but about the two things Clarke seems to think we mortals would most like to know in a universe in which we can only hope that the odds are in favor of the race's survival: that we are not alone and that we have not lived in vain.

Comment on *2001* has tended to concentrate on the film, using the novel only as a sort of aid to explication, especially of the ending; which has prompted more than one critic to complain that a film ending that needs a novel to explain it is not a success. And in fact commentators have tended to think that the film's ending is a failure.

General consideration of the film seems to me to take one of two tacks. It is either read as an attack upon humans who have become machines, or it is seen as a celebration of the human triumph over the machine within ourselves. Either way, the central focus is not on the fetus at the end but on the machine in the middle.

Norman Kagan, while acknowledging that the film may be

seen as a "new myth" which, like the old myths, makes "man at least potentially the center of the universe," really finds the last third of it "curiously weak," capable only of giving him a feeling of "meaninglessness and futility." The "Star-Child floats in space beside the earth, enormous-eyed, ethereal," but also "passive, aloof, hesitant." "Compare this," he suggests, "with the shambling, daring, and then masterful joyousness of the tool-using man-ape."

Whether such a comparison is fair or not, the best-realized part of the film becomes from such a point of view the middle. Hal is the "super-rational" tool, the embodiment of an "ideal state" toward which humans have been yearning so much that their lives are "sapped of vigor, wonder, or even meaning." When Hal "begins to acquire emotions, an ego, and the beginning of a personality," he recognizes "his own emptiness" as the humans do not recognize theirs. He becomes, as several critics have claimed, more human than the film's humans.

Daniel De Vries, on the other hand, while acknowledging that Kubrick's humans "are all too believable technocrats," argues that just "as the man-apes had run into a dead end, barely scraping by in the desert, so twenty-first-century man has come to a dead end in 2001, losing his soul, and now control of his destiny, to his technology. Perhaps the point of the whole HAL business is that Bowman, in battling HAL and winning, reasserts the integrity of mankind."

Critics who do concentrate on Clarke's *2001* may be, it seems to me, similarly divided. There are those who think the book is a "mature amalgamation" of Clarke's "interest in scientific detail" and his "commitment to a homocentric and optimistic vision" (Eric S. Rabkin). And there are others who complain that the book's symbols are "murky as philosophy" and "empty as human experience" (George Edgar Slusser). They say the novel "does not make it clear why, if technological progress itself delights him as much as it seems to, Clarke should find the transcendent state necessary" (John Huntington).

Rabkin argues that Clarke's concerns for "science and vision" are brought together in the invention of the monolith. He traces various towers in Clarke's previous stories, saying they represent "knowledge and power and communication"—"science, in short." These he connects with the phallic nature of such towers generally to say that in the monolith Clarke found a symbol that put together for him both science and the progress of the generations toward a "new spiritual perspective."

(Rabkin also says that Clarke's *2001* reminds him of Olaf Stapledon's novels. He probably means *Star Maker* rather than *Last and First Men*, and in so saying he echoes the opinion of several critics that Clarke's Star-Child owes much to Stapledon's Star Maker. But I remain unconvinced, as I said in the first chapter, that Stapledon's influence is any more important in understanding Clarke than is the whole movement of more optimistic thought on the same matters which can be represented by the end of Tennyson's *In Memoriam*, by the claim that the child conceived tonight is the next step between us and the "one far-off divine event, / To which creation moves.")

Slusser argues that "both Moon-Watcher and Hal—ape and machine—do not evolve so much as fall." "Moon-Watcher's people once enjoyed an Edenic past—warm rains and lush fertility." The monolith "teaches him to kill for food"; "he teaches himself to kill for power." Hal is born in an "electronic Eden" and "is corrupted and led to killing by a split programmed into him—the disparity between truth and lie, ideal and real world."

Bowman travels "to the limits of human possibility," but finds only a "hotel room." The Star-Child "goes back to an Earth so polluted that the only 'cleaning' possible is destruction." The "encounter with the alien" is "an encounter with our own fallen selves," "trapped between ape and god." The novel is "clearly skeptical" of "man's capacities in the face of cosmic mystery"; Clarke's "lyrical dignity gives way to satire," his characters' "elegaic nobility to something closer to foolish impotence."

My own position is a good deal closer to that of Thomas D. Clareson, who argues that *2001* the novel can best be understood by coming at it from the four rejected stories that make up *The Lost Worlds of 2001* (1972). There visiting extraterrestrials decide "to intervene" in the development of the "hominids" they find on Earth. "Left to themselves," says Clareson, the man-apes "would have little chance of survival, for 'the universe [is] as indifferent to intelligence as it [is] to life.' "

The extraterrestrials leave "a signaling device" on the Moon, for " 'only a spacefaring culture could truly transcend its environment and join others in giving a purpose to creation.' " "Clarke makes," according to Clareson, "no more succinct statement of his central dream. Yet it is a dream hardpressed by anxiety, 'for if the stars and the Galaxies [have] the least concern for mind, or the least awareness of its presence, that [is] yet to be proved.' "

I would only add that in *2001* as published the step has been taken. Humanity has become what Clareson and the rejected stories only suggest is possible: "part of a community of intelligence which alone gives meaning to the indifferent splendor of the Universe." The dream is presented as having been true all along.

Some sense of how far Clarke has come from the pessimism of Wells (and Stapledon) can be had from a comparison of *2001* the novel with the earlier story that was its germ, "The Sentinel" (1951). In that story the veteran of several years of Moon exploration comes upon a "pyramidal structure" in the mountains that surround the Sea of Crises. The find is a signaling device left on the Moon long "before life had emerged from the seas of Earth." Since then it has been patiently reporting the fact that it has not yet been found.

The extraterrestrials who left the pyramid "must have searched the star-clusters as we have searched the planets," says the explorer. The "smoke of the great volcanoes" must have still been "staining the skies" when the "first ship of the peoples of the dawn came sliding in from the abyss beyond Pluto. It passed the frozen outer worlds, knowing that life could play no part in their destinies. It came to rest among the inner planets, warming themselves around the fire of the Sun and waiting for their stories to begin.

"Those wanderers must have looked on Earth, circling safely in the narrow zone between fire and ice, and must have guessed that it was the favorite of the Sun's children."

In one sense the story rests on the contrast between the ordinariness of frying breakfast sausages, as the narrator is doing when he first catches sight of the reflected light that leads him to the pyramid, and the extraordinary final discovery that the device was left long ago by another star's far more advanced civilization. It is the Wellsian theme that we are not the root and crown of things.

For me, however, almost every moment of the story is shot through with the awareness of the fragility of life. I cannot read the quotation given above without noticing the "narrow zone between fire and ice," without being aware that the analogy of children warming themselves at a fire may imply ghost stories, without being reminded that away from the Sun is "the abyss beyond Pluto." Just calling the histories of planets "stories" implies that there are endings, and the reference to the "peoples of the dawn" is a reminder that there will be an evening and a night as well. To me this story has the equally Wellsian insistence that we are not invulnerable.

The story's central discovery is the pyramid, but that shape itself is suggestive of a civilization long dead (which is one of the reasons Clarke and Kubrick decided not to use it in *2001*). And the find is made against the bleakest of backgrounds, a Moon on which, we are regularly told, primitive life forms were "already dying" just as they were "beginning on

Earth." The explorer's first thought, for that matter, is the gleeful assumption that the pyramid is an Egyptian-like relic of a civilization on the Moon. "I felt a great lifting of my heart. . . . For I loved the Moon, and now I knew that the creeping moss of Aristarchus and Eratosthenes was not the only life she had brought forth in her youth. The old, discredited dream of the first explorers was true. There had, after all, been a lunar civilization." The idea of ruins is so tied in with the idea of end that the picture he imagines of that civilization is of its last days. He sees the priests of that culture "calling on their gods to preserve them as the life of the Moon ebbed with the dying oceans, and calling on their gods in vain."

The device is not a ruin but a signal, and so the story does say that there is intelligent—even more intelligent—life somewhere in the universe. But the device is also called a "sentinel," even "a fire alarm" after humans have smashed it with their atomic tools. The story ends, not as does *2001* with the sense that the peoples of the dawn are benevolent, but with two threats upon our own survival: that we may destroy ourselves and that we may be destroyed. "Perhaps you understand now why that crystal pryamid was set upon the Moon instead of on the Earth. Its builders were not concerned with races still struggling up from savagery. They would be interested in our civilization only if we proved our fitness to survive —by crossing space and so escaping from the Earth, our cradle. That is the challenge that all intelligent races must meet, sooner or later. It is a double challenge, for it depends in turn upon the conquest of atomic energy and the last choice between life and death." And as for those peoples of the dawn themselves: "Perhaps they wish to help our infant civilization. But they must be very, very old, and the old are often insanely jealous of the young."

It may be that we are to assume that by 2016, the year in which the story is told to us, humans will have learned to avoid atomic self-destruction (though the destruction of the pyramid with atomic tools raises doubts about this); it is even possible to speculate, as does Robert Plank in discussing this story, that the narrator's fear of the peoples of the dawn is a reflection of humanity's youth. But what the story says to me is that space is wide and time is long, that civilizations can miss each other as easily in the one as in the other, and that life comes and goes and sometimes never gets to be. All we can do at the end of the story is "wait," which was all we could do before the pyramid was found. At best "The Sentinel" says only that we may not have to wait so hopelessly; at least two races may find each other in the abyss. And even that hope has something in it of the picture the explorer summons up of the last days of the Moon's civilization—calling to their gods and calling in vain.

9

... the Stars

AS the TV picture from the probe they have dropped into Jupiter's atmosphere flickers and goes out, Clarke's Bowman and Poole ask themselves how humans will ever explore that giant planet. What kind of machines, they wonder, can protect frail human bodies from those pressures and that gravity?

Clarke's *2001* seems to answer that humans will evolve beyond such physical limitations, that our descendants will be able to travel anywhere in the cosmos at will. In the years since that novel, however, Clarke has played his cards much closer to his vest. He has concentrated on the more immediate future, on a humanity not yet either succeeded by machinery or evolved into pure consciousness. And because he has so concentrated, because he has allowed those alternatives, even the suggestion that the consciousness may follow the machine, to remain only possibilities, to be, as they are in most of his fiction, the potential but ultimately unknowable future, his recent fiction offers a useful statement of his work's central hope: the hope that the human race will not have lived in vain. The specific nature of humanity's future, after all, does not matter. What matters is the hope that our passing, if our species must pass, will not be as meaningless as the passing of the dinosaurs seems to have been. What matters is that intelligence seem to have a chance in the universe. What matters is that our desire to know and to understand was a right direction, that we were at least a branch of the central evolutionary tree.

One answer to Bowman's and Poole's question about how Jupiter is to be explored is offered by the story "A Meeting with Medusa" (1971). In it, the giant planet is explored—in part at least—by Howard Falcon, a man more closely partnered with machinery than the astronauts of either version of *2001*, a man who, although he feels himself outgrowing his race, is still human enough to share our aspirations, who suggests, in fact, that our descendants, whatever their nature, will still share at least our curiosity, our desire to understand.

When we first meet Falcon, he is the captain of a giant dirigible which is about to be wrecked—in spite of "multiple-redundancy, fail-safe takeovers, and any number of back-up systems." The problem is, as Falcon explains later, "time lag." The operator of a remote-controlled flying camera fails to realize that his commands are being routed through a satellite and are thus subject to a "half-second time lag." It is as if he were driving "a car over a bumpy road with a half-second delay in the steering." The result is that the camera tears into the airship and brings it down, its fall a replay of that of the *Hindenburg* "a century and a half before."

As Falcon looks up at the light coming through the tear the camera makes in the dirigible's fabric, he is for a split second reminded of standing in the nave of a great cathedral. This time, however, the cathedral has a metal frame and is falling down out of the sky. The old religion of humanity—in this case its faith that it can use its machines to explore the universe—is collapsing. What is needed is a much closer marriage of human and machine.

When the doctors put Howard Falcon together again, he is a cyborg, a human brain with a mechanical body. As such he can go where humans cannot, he can bring into play "skill and experience and swift reactions," things that cannot "yet be programed into a computer." He is sent—in another balloon —into the atmosphere of Jupiter, in part because he asks to be, but mainly because he can function there. Properly strapped in, he is "virtually a part of the ship's structure."

The balance of the story is about Falcon's brief flight into the upper levels of Jupiter's sky, a description of what he sees there and especially of a life form he meets. But it is also a study of how difficult it is to know anything with any certainty, how confusing the evidence is and how unclear the categories.

When Falcon sees bars of light flashing toward him, he wonders if they may be a sign of some intelligence taking notice of him. The "pattern" of the lights is "so regular—so *artificial.*" The lights turn out, however, to be produced by shock waves from a volcanolike eruption, a phenomenon similar to the "Wheels of Poseidon" produced in the seas of Earth by underwater earthquakes.

When Falcon hears, on the other hand, a noise that "booms" regularly, a noise that the scientists in Mission Control decide *"must"* be the sound of some natural phenomenon, "a waterfall," "a geyser," "a stormy sea," the truth turns out to be that the booms are made by gigantic jellyfishlike creatures floating in Jupiter's atmosphere, the medusae of the title, animals "a hundred thousand times larger" than whales (Mission Control had thought, since the sound waves were "a hundred yards long," that even "an animal as big as a whale couldn't produce them"). Earth's categories, to put it another way, both do and do not apply to the giant planet. The medusae are like jellyfish, but they are also many times larger than the largest animals we have ever seen.

That the medusae, being like jellyfish, also resemble Falcon's balloon is very much to the point. The medusae seem to have developed naturally the ability to tune in on radio waves, something animals on Earth, though some of them have "sonar and even electric senses," "never got around to doing." On Earth, it was humans who learned to use radio waves; Falcon sticks his antennas out the side of his balloon capsule, the medusae have grown theirs on their sides. The point being that, in the long view, there is no difference between evolution and invention: it is no less "natural" for humans to have developed antennas through invention than it is for the medusae to have developed them through evolution.

If there is no difference between evolution and invention, then the making of a cyborg is not unnatural; it is just an evolutionary next step. Falcon is no freak; he is just the first man to have his frail flesh replaced by a manufactured body. He is as afloat on the winds of change, in as much of a controlled drift, as he is in his balloon in Jupiter's atmosphere.

The nature of reality is presented in this story, as it is to a certain extent in *Childhood's End* and *2001*, by a volcano and a huge whirlwind, both on the surface of Jupiter. As Falcon contemplates both, as he thinks of the sheer size of the planet, he feels "a wind colder than the atmosphere around him . . . blowing through his soul." The universe may never, he thinks, echoing the Overlords of *Childhood's End*, "be a place for man." "Perhaps" such "air-breathing, radiation-sensitive bundles of unstable carbon compounds" "should stick to their natural homes."

The universe may prove no place for humans. Or, again as in *Childhood's End* or *2001*, humans may have to change so much that we would no longer recognize them. Either way, the story seems to argue, it is natural to evolve in the direction of staying afloat in the cold winds of existence.

Falcon has been troubled by nightmare memories of being brought back to life, of being reborn as a machine-man. Similarly, he has been unable to get out of his mind the "super-chimps," the "simps," who went down with his dirigible. He had always felt a "strange mingling of kinship and discomfort" when he looked into the eyes of those near-humans (who had been developed to do routine tasks aboard the airship). By the end of the story, however, he has been able to come to terms with his similar situation, with his being "between two worlds" as is the simp. He now accepts "his role" as the link "between the creatures of carbon and the creatures of metal who must replace them."

George Edgar Slusser has called Falcon's feelings of being an outsider "Byronic posturing." But I think the machine-man is presented with more sympathy than that (if I may use Clarke's own play on simp). Falcon comes to his sense of being alone and separate as we come to the knowledge that we must die. He is content—as we must be—if he can believe that he may not have lived in vain.

Rendezvous with Rama (1973) is the story of humanity's investigation of an enormous alien spaceship, a spinning cylinder fifty kilometers tall, which whirls through our solar system, draws energy from our Sun, and departs. What the novel does to summarize Clarke's fiction is to repeat again the difference between that fiction and the pessimism represented by Wells' scientific romances. When Wells' "Star" whirls through our solar system, it causes catastrophic damage, not only to Earth but also to humanity's picture of itself as important in the universe. Clarke's cylinder, on the other hand, while taking no more notice of the human race than does Wells' star, is occasion to celebrate humanity's urge to know, to remind ourselves that the race is not yet dead, that we may still be more important in the universe than the pessimists suggest.

The book has much to say about the difficulties of humans learning anything about the universe. The scientists who advise—from the safety of the Moon—the investigators inside the alien spaceship are all too old and too set in their opinions to be of much help. The investigation itself is epitomized by the brief and only partially successful flight of an incredibly fragile glider from one end of the spaceship to the other. And certainly the stairway "as high as the Himalayas" which leads from the ship's air lock to its floor "invalidates," as Eric S. Rabkin has said, "the idea that man is the measure of things." The stairway "broods," as Rabkin goes on to say, over the novel's "tiny humans exploring a world vastly bigger than themselves." The humans crawl along the circle cast by their spotlight in the total dark of the ship's interior, and cannot help but think of themselves as insects inside a giant bottle.

And as if sheer size were not enough, the novel also repeatedly points out that humans cannot trust their own minds. They make false analogies based on previous experience, leap to conclusions not justified, and think in categories that do not apply. They cast their own shadows ahead of them, as they do walking in the circle of the spotlight, and read that projection as the truth about the makers of the alien vessel.

But the point is that humans can still discover the truth. They are often wrong—short-sighted and set in their ways— but there is enough truth in their categories and analogies to enable them to make several correct conjectures about the huge cylinder they call Rama. The ship's lights do come on in what can be interpreted as a dawn, the nearness of the passage to the Sun does warm the vessel into a kind of spring, and the life process that begins, that produces the machine-animals that perform a quick maintenance check of the ship, is a speeded-up form of evolution. Even the fact that the cylinder turns out to be a sort of "space ark," carrying the disembodied patterns of its builders, makes the name Rama, the name of one of the incarnations of the Hindu god Vishnu the Preserver, more appropriate than the humans who chose it anticipated. The book is not, as George Edgar Slusser claims, a presentation of "man" as "the stupid tourist before the mysteries of the universe"; it is instead an argument that we are increasing our understanding, that we do—awkwardly, with great difficulty, and even accidentally—build on previous knowledge. The book is about, as Eric S. Rabkin suggests, our desire to understand even a universe that does "not care" whether it is "understood."

The chief thing in trying to understand Rama, decides Commander William Norton, the novel's protagonist, is not to let it "overwhelm him." He has had, while exploring the floor (wall) of the gigantic spinning cylinder, a sense of déjà vu which momentarily turns his "well-ordered universe" "upside down," which gives him "a dizzying glimpse" of "mysteries at the edge of existence." It turns out, not that Commander Norton has been inside Rama before, but—as in most cases of déjà vu—that he has a half-remembered similar experience in his childhood. More to the point, the explanation does not deny the fact that there are mysteries to Rama; it argues that it is not yet clear by any means that the mysteries of Rama are "beyond human understanding." The situation is like the moment when Norton is on the giant staircase and Rama's lights come on. For a few seconds, because he seems suspended miles above the vessel's floor, he panics. Then, looking at his position from another angle, realizing that he is in the zero gravity of the cylinder's hub, he sees how much of his fear is related to his way of looking at the ship's Brobdingnagian interior. The exploratory expedition inside Rama, for that matter, has several such moments of optical illusion beyond which humans have to force themselves to see. All people can do, faced with the size of the cosmos and the limits to their own ways of seeing, is what the names of the two human-built ships in the novel—the *Resolution* and the *Endeavour*—advise them to do: they can resolve and endeavor to continue to try to understand the universe.

The novel is also about refraining from the unnecessary use of force. Commander Norton puts off for as long as he can the use of lasers to cut into the covering the Ramans have used to protect much of the inside of Rama. He is a little apprehensive about the precautions such an advanced civilization may have taken to protect its property, but for the most part he does "not wish to behave like a technological barbarian, smashing what he [cannot] understand." When he does open one of the storage buildings, he hopes the Ramans will "forgive him" and "understand that it was all in the cause of science."

The distinction between using a little force in the pursuit of knowledge and refraining from unnecessary force is made clear by the repeated image of a hammer blow. Norton does not exert his full strength when what turns out to be one of Rama's lights gives only "a dull, unmusical 'clunk' " in answer to a gentle tap of his hammer. He does not want to "be like a vandal smashing some enormous plate-glass window." However, when the ship's medical officer, Dr. Laura Ernst, finds that what looks like ice is in fact ice, she does not hesitate to strike it with her hammer in order to gather "a few cc's" of Rama's water.

The image of a hammer blow has even larger implications. The book opens with a brief history of Earth's recent experience with meteorites, climaxing with the destruction of much of northern Italy by "a thousand tons of rock and metal" "moving at fifty kilometers a second." The disaster is called a "hammer blow from space." Later in the novel, when the humans who live on Mercury decide to destroy Rama with an atomic rocket because they fear it means to go into orbit around the Sun and dominate the system, the bomb is described as looking like a hammer, indeed as being "a hammer, one powerful enough to smash a world."

Commander Norton decides to disconnect the bomb, in part because he does not believe the Ramans mean humanity ill, and, more important, because "survival is not everything." To allow the bomb to be used against the ship would be to say that there is no difference between the human race and the unthinking universe.

But I have gotten away from my point. I started out to say that *Rendezvous with Rama* is a useful restatement of the difference between Clarke's fiction and the tradition represented by Wells' scientific romances. And *Rendezvous with Rama* certainly is Clarke's most conscious statement about the fiction that gave his fiction birth.

Early in the story, just after Rama has been discovered at the edge of the solar system, Clarke has an astronomer be reminded of Wells' "The Star." Clarke has his astronomer remember that Wells' story is about "another visitor from the stars," one that smashes into Neptune, bursts with it into flame —into a star—and causes great devastation on Earth as it falls inward to the Sun. Clarke's astronomer wonders if Rama may not be a "collapsed star," "a madly spinning sphere of neutronium, every cubic centimeter" of which weighs "billions of tons." If so, then even though it is "a cold body," the visitor from deep space will be able to kill by gravity as easily as Wells' "star" killed "by fire." Rama could "completely distort the orbits of the planets," and it would take a move of only "a few million kilometers" for the "delicate balance" of the Earth's climate "to be destroyed."

In one sense, this idea—which Clarke's astronomer immediately rejects because Rama has not had any influence on the orbits of the outer planets—is simply Clarke's statement of how he might use a collapsed star—a black hole if you will— to rewrite Wells' story. In a more important sense, however, *Rendezvous with Rama* as it is written is an answer to Wells' "The Star." Wells' story has, as I pointed out in the first chapter, a mathematician who is able to say that he understands the random and uncaring nature of the universe because he understands the implications of "the star" smashing its way through the solar system like a billiard ball. Clarke's novel, on the other hand, is not so sure. It focuses, not on an astronomer, but on Commander Norton, a man not much concerned with the ultimate nature of reality, but much troubled at the end of the book because "the nature and the purpose of the Ramans" remains "utterly unknown."

The difference is not just between the far and the near, the certain and the uncertain. It is more centrally between those who emphasize the universe's apparent unconcern and those who try, albeit somewhat desperately, to emphasize the accomplishments of intelligence. It is a difference represented in the novel by the statements of two astronomers, one of whom might be a descendant of Wells' astronomer, the other more Clarkeian in outlook. The Wellsian considers "the activity of intelligent life" to be "an unfortunate irrelevance in the majestic universe of stars and galaxies." The more Clarkeian astronomer is convinced that "the only purpose of the universe" is "the production of intelligence"; everything else is "mere dead matter."

The final truth, of course, remains as yet unknowable. Insofar as Rama sails away, as it does, without in any way acknowledging the existence of the human race, it remains a symbol of the universe's indifference. Insofar, however, as it is itself a magnificent achievement, a triumph over the vast depths of time and space, it is a symbol of the power of intelligence to deal in and perhaps even *with* the universe.

The novel ends with a scene in which Commander William Norton and Dr. Laura Ernst make love. Although Norton is married (has two wives, in fact, one on Mars and one on Earth), the two ship's officers have embraced before, "on Earth, long ago, in a moment of mutual loneliness and depression." This seems to be a similar occasion. Norton had expected from Rama "some dramatic, even transcendental, revelation," but now, since it has left the system, he fears that "the rest of his life" will "be haunted by a sense of anticlimax and the knowledge of opportunities missed." He feels the human search for truth is not badly represented by a dream he has of "climbing an infinite stairway." The lovemaking, then, is, as it is in *A Fall of Moondust*, a protest against the impersonality of the universe. And Norton knows that "the end-of-mission 'orbital orgy' " is probably going on all over the ship.

But the novel offers another possibility in addition to this scene of human love as comforting. Dr. Ernst had come to Norton's cabin to tell him that she has just received word that his request for another child has been granted, that his wife on Mars is probably being artificially inseminated "right now" (since "radiation-induced mutation" is a "certainty" for spacemen, he was "sterilized when he entered the service" and a supply of his sperm frozen). The thought of that conception may have something to do with what takes place between the two officers, but, more important, Norton's child, mentioned as it is in the book's last chapter, becomes the symbol of humanity's continued existence. It combines with the references to the Ramans' fondness for triple redundancy—to the fact that they "do everything in threes," as the novel's last line emphasizes—to argue that there will be other ships, that the human race will have future chances to increase its knowledge.

Imperial Earth (1976) is about a young pioneer who returns to Earth from his home on Titan, one of Saturn's moons, in 2276, the United States' quincentennial year. What the novel does in summary of Clarke's fiction, however, is to repeat both the argument against trying to halt change (as it is articulated in, for example, *The City and the Stars*) and the teasing hope that humanity's intuitions about the universe may be in some sense true (as they are, for example, in *Childhood's End*).

The novel's protagonist, Duncan Makenzie, the youngest member of Titan's ruling clan, returns to Earth to make political contacts. But he also comes to have a clone made from his genes. He has to do so because he has inherited, although he is himself a clone, the results of his grandfather's years in space. The Makenzies cannot sire healthy children.

The advantage of cloning, as the doctor to whom Duncan applies says, is that it comes closer than do ordinary children to dealing with "the problem of succession." One can "improve the odds" that a "dynasty" will continue along desired lines if one leaves behind "a carbon copy" of oneself. Cloning is, as another doctor says, a kind of "immortality."

The difficulties with such immortality are made clear in the book. Titan itself, which was settled because its great supplies of hydrogen could be used to refuel spaceships, has about ten years to change completely the basis of its economy. In the future, ships will be powered by a sort of drive that totally annihilates its fuel and thus needs much less. Similarly, on Earth, the small sea creatures which were bred to absorb gold out of the ocean have been rendered obsolete by nuclear furnaces that can "manufacture gold as cheaply as any other metal." And the novel's climax takes place at the site of Cyclops, the giant radio system built to listen for signals from deep space, which is about to be replaced by the new boon to Titan's economy, Argus, a listening device to be built out beyond Saturn. The Makenzies' attempt to stop change, in other words, is seen against a background that emphasizes the fact that change is inevitable.

When Duncan finds out that his former friend and lover Karl Helmer, the scion of Titan's second most powerful family, is on Earth raising money, he fears a coup d'état. But when Karl, who is really trying to raise money for the Argus listening device, asks Duncan how the latter's grandfather, the original settler of Titan, got his start, built his fortune, the question focuses Duncan's doubts, some of which he already had, about the legitimacy of the Makenzies' urge to perpetuate themselves.

The young man admits as much when he says, at the quincentennial celebration, that it is possible to have an "unhealthy preoccupation with the past." He is too well mannered to make it clear that he is referring to Earth, to the civilization he has found to be epitomized by the preserved luxury of the *Titanic*, raised from her grave on the Grand Banks. But he is also referring to his family's desire to have him cloned, to an "obsession with the past" which is in danger of becoming like that he finds on Earth.

The novel's most powerful example of the unhealthiness of being preoccupied with the past is the memory both Duncan and Karl have of the adolescent love affair they had, at the same time, with Calindy Ellerman, a lovely young visitor to Titan from Earth. Duncan has a picture of her which she gave to him as a going-away present. The pictured smile, however —appropriately enough, for she much preferred Karl—seems directed at someone over his shoulder. This dual rejection, by Karl as well as by Calindy, has conditioned not only his relationship with the former, but also, to a lesser extent, his ability to love the woman, as beautiful as Calindy, who has become his wife.

The unhealthiness of Karl's memory, on the other hand, reminds one of Clark's earlier fiction, of "The Lion of Comarre" as well as of *The City and the Stars*. The last time Calindy and Karl make love, having slipped away from Duncan, she allows him to use "an emotion amplifier." The result is that Karl, who uses the machine at full power, cannot either forget her or love anyone else. He finds that his memory of the experience "makes real life seem pale and thin." He turns away from Duncan because he is no more able than are the dreamers in Comarre to live amid the imperfections of ordinary life. He leaves behind, in the notebook Duncan reads after his death, a drawing of the young Calindy as they "both" remember her, as "the girl frozen forever" "beyond the reach of Time."

When Duncan visits Calindy on Earth, fifteen years after the affair, he finds that she is still given to flirting with enhanced experience. Not only is she the vice president of a company that furnishes planned adventures to bored Earthlings, but she also hands Duncan a "tactoid," an egg-shaped object which, when he closes his eyes and holds it, gives him a "kaleidoscope" of sensations, from sandpaper to satin. She does it in order to give him some idea of what the "joy machine" did to Karl, but for all of her experience, for all of the fact that she is a thoroughly believable *femme fatale*, she is still half innocent. She has never understood, because she did not use the machine at full power, Karl's passion for her, his desperate need to come to Earth to be with her. She could not help being flattered by it, but she never understood it.

Time takes its toll, of course. When Karl gets to Earth, he finds that the mature Calindy, though still a very desirable woman, cannot live up to his memory. She, in turn, is made to feel "inadequate," is reminded of her own "lost youth"; they fight and part. Duncan too, when he and Calindy console each other after Karl's accidental death, finds that she no longer seems to taste of honey. Clarke has drawn upon, to put it another way, all the power latent in the idea of our remembering our past loves, not to exclude all the suspicion that the other did not suffer quite so much and all of the later certainty that we probably caused ourselves the pain, to underline the truth that we can "never quite recover the past."

But let me repeat that Duncan is predisposed to decide against cloning. He is disdainful of tourists who cannot go anywhere without their "voice-activated recorders," who have to make permanent what they say or what is said to them. And when he has a nightmare about being sucked into the tiny Black Hole that is the new space drive, it is not total annihilation he fears, but the infinite extension of time that may take place at the edge of such a phenomenon: he imagines the "passing seconds" becoming "longer" and "longer" and himself "trapped forever in a changeless Eternity." He is, from the beginning of the book, ready to agree with the doctor who refuses to do the cloning, who says that since the "genes are no longer shuffled," it "means the end of biological progress."

The novel's other major theme is introduced by the puzzle, the set of pentominoes, given to Duncan as he is leaving for Earth. He has known the game since he was ten, has been told in fact that "it is very much more than a game." And the various ways rectangular arrangements can be made of the twelve five-sided pieces do open to the ten-year-old Duncan "endless vistas and horizons." They suggest, since they may be said to "create a universe," that the larger universe may be similarly solvable.

The more immediate lesson of the game comes when the young Duncan challenges the then fifteen-year-old Karl with one of the more difficult arrangements, a task that would take a computer working at a move a second "rather more than six million, *million years.*" Karl solves it overnight, and that gives Duncan his "first glimpse of the power of intuition," of "the mind's mysterious ability to go beyond the available facts and to short-circuit the process of logic."

The novel insists that we "all" have, to some degree, the ability to do, as Karl does, something a machine cannot. Be that as it may, this celebration of an intuitive leap makes it clear, as does Bowman's skipping of the machine stage at the end of *2001*, that Clarke's sympathies are not fully engaged by the idea that evolution's next step is the machine. That possible future is just one of many, one particularly useful in deflating humanity's pretensions, but one accepted with resignation even by Howard Falcon, the machine-man of "A Meeting with Medusa."

More to the point, the importance of intuition's success in the novel is hinted at by a minor character's exclaiming that "coincidences are fascinating," that he has been "collecting them" all his life. The novel itself collects coincidences and uses them to suggest that reality may have underlying correspondences and connections which are what intuition gets at. (In a note, Clarke says that he read Arthur Koestler's *The Roots of Coincidence* only after he had finished writing *Imperial Earth*, but he also acknowledges that that is a coincidence even he finds difficult to believe.)

When Duncan sees his first honeycomb (on Earth; there are no bees on Titan), he is reminded, by the taste of honey, of Calindy. When he begins to flip through Karl's notebook he gets beyond human relationships and into questions about the organization of the universe. He finds a "honeycomb pattern" in the midst of several "geometrical doodles" "based on the hexagon motif." He recognizes it as a diagram of the radio telescope, Cyclops, which he now knows Karl was studying.

But he also recognizes the other hexagons, some of which dwindle "away into the distance," as the "lattice" to be found inside the mysterious material "titanite."

The correspondence is important because both Cyclops and the hexagons inside the strange material seem to open on the infinite. One of the central pieces in Duncan's set of pentominoes is made of titanite, and he remembers that when he looked at the piece under a microscope he saw a "hexagonal corridor of light, dwindling away to infinity." He could, by changing the focus, "hurtle down that corridor, without ever coming to an end." He was moved to marvel how "incredible" it is that "such a universe" lies "inside a piece of rock." Karl even argues that the material is not "natural," that it could not just "*happen*." It must be, he thinks, a record of an extraterrestrial interpretation of the universe.

The book does not go so far. It only has Duncan pause—in one of the last scenes—before a large model of the DNA helix (itself discovered by an intuitive leap, as we all know from James D. Watson's *The Double Helix*). Duncan is reminded of his pentominoes because he knows that, although there are "only twelve" of those five-sided shapes, "it would take the lifetime of the universe to exhaust their possibilities." Here there is "no mere dozen, but billions upon billions of locations to be filled by the letters of the genetic code." And yet both the puzzle and the helix have been in part understood and in part controlled by human minds.

But the most impressive correspondence as far as Duncan is concerned, the one that gives him such a strong sense of déjà vu that he begins to believe somewhat in destiny, is the last drawing in Karl's notebook. It is a sketch of a new radio telescope, of Argus, but Duncan thinks it is a "detailed study" of a "spiny sea urchin" which he first saw just a few days before. When Duncan approached the sea creature, it swung its "long spines" toward him, orienting itself "in the direction of maximum danger." And such, as Duncan later discovers, is, in a real sense, the way Argus will work. The little creature

was "scanning" its universe "as Argus would search the stars."
Duncan has "not been vouchsafed some blinding revelation, like an ancient prophet receiving the word of God." All
that has happened is that he has "come across the same very
unusual shape in two quite independent contexts." But he has
experienced:

> that indescribable shock a man may know only once in a
> lifetime, when he is in the presence of the transcendental
> and feels the sure foundations of his world and his philosophy trembling beneath his feet.

When he saw that careful drawing in Karl's sketchbook, Duncan had recognized it at once. But now it
seemed to him that the recognition came not only from
the past, but also from the future. It was as if he had
caught a momentary glimpse in the Mirror of Time, reflecting something that had not yet occurred—and something that must be awesomely important for it to have
succeeded in reversing the flow of causality.

Project Argus was part of the destiny of mankind; of
this, Duncan was now sure beyond any need for rational
proof.

Calindy is the vice president of a firm called Enigma, whose
motto is: "We astonish." The central enigma of the novel,
however, is represented by the coincidence of the two shapes,
the small sea creature and the giant radio telescope. That
correspondence astonishes Duncan, makes him wonder if
everything is not as fated as the *Titanic* and its iceberg seem
almost to have been. The "greatest mystery of all" is that we
are occasionally so astonished. It would not be surprising, especially in a meaningless universe, if we were never teased
with the possibility of meaning. What is surprising, especially
in a universe whose meaning—if there is one—is uncertain,
is that on occasion we think we see behind the veil, into the
heart of things. We should be glad of such moments of aston-

ishment, Duncan says in his quincentennial speech: they suggest that we may have "great goals beyond ourselves." Such moments help us get beyond the inevitable disappointments of human relationships; they hint that the universe may be a puzzle after all, that it may have a solution.

There is no necessary reason why the solution to the universe—or even the intermediate solutions along the way—should amount to good news for humanity. When Duncan hears Karl's tapes of the sort of sound waves Argus is to capture, he is unable to tell whether he is listening to something alive or manufactured or natural. The "sound," like the sound Howard Falcon hears in "A Meeting with Medusa," might be "the slow beating of a giant heart," "or the tolling of a bell," or "the waves of the sea, rolling forever in unvarying rhythm against some desolate shore." In fact, in that the matter leaving the universe through the new space drive does so with a "thin wail" which Duncan interprets as its "death cry," in that when Duncan kills the sea urchin he is aware of its "death rattle," there is much reason—many correspondences and coincidences—to believe Karl's "last awesome intuition," that the sound waves are produced by "Star Beasts" who may be either "gods" or the "EATERS OF GODS."

The book argues that humanity must "face the truth, whatever it might be and wherever it might lead." Even the desire for immortality, which hope Duncan rejects for himself, is treated sympathetically in that Duncan understands why people would want to win the *Titanic* back from the sea. He is not surprised by Earth's efforts to rebreed wolves and even, it is rumored, dinosaurs. He himself worries about the three backup embryos which are not used when, in the novel's major turnaround, he decides to have a clone made from Karl's dead body. The difference seems to be that worrying about the embryos is worrying about unrealized potential, not trying to recover the past; it is choosing the best future for Titan rather than the dead past of the *Titanic*.

Let me try to be clearer. Cloning, it turns out in the novel, is, like atomic power, "neither good nor bad"; "only its purpose [is] important." Cloning is used, not to bring back the dead Karl, but to create a second Karl, a genius who may this time escape from the obsession with the personal and discover for the human race a bit more of the truth. The power of science, which cloning represents, may be used to cooperate with the best direction for the species, may help humans to see, as Duncan sees, that in an important sense the film of an atomic blast may be thought of as a film of a sunset run backward, that such awesome power may be used to put off the race's nightfall. What is gotten rid of by cloning is not, as the Makenzies hoped, the threat of death and change; what is gotten rid of is humanity's inability to think of itself as one, our inability to be other than selfish. What Duncan does in giving up his family's future for the race's future is, as Eugene Tanzy has said of this novel, to accept the possibilities, even the frightening possibilities, of change. What he does is to declare that humanity will act as if the universe is a puzzle, as if the obligation of all of us is to aid in the solution of it.

Duncan's decision to have Karl cloned is seen against a background in which the human race has clearly grown closer together. Most of the people on Titan either are or act as if they are related to each other. Duncan's host on Earth, George Washington, is a descendant of Cabots, Du Ponts, Kennedys, Kissingers, and "a couple of African kings." Duncan himself, in spite of his Scottish name, is a black man. Even the Daughters of the American Revolution has become an organization of ladies whose forefathers were not just at Yorktown or Valley Forge, but "fought in the hills with Castro, or accompanied Mao on the Long March, or shared the sealed train with Lenin, or [fell] in the final assault on Cape Town." It has become a group whose membership testifies to the universality of revolution, of change.

The sexual customs the novel takes for granted are also a sign of oneness. Duncan and Karl assume it is perfectly normal to have affairs with both sexes, that anyone who does not is "polarized." Such is not presented as a sign of decadence, but as a sign of unity, of the greater good for which Duncan acts.

Finally, Duncan's decision to have Karl cloned is his attempt to balance himself between the two pieces of advice he is regularly given, the advice to master the "administration of the unforeseen" and the almost contrary advice to "co-operate with the inevitable." He is, as Clarke's protagonists regularly are, riding the waves on his own kind of surfboard.

In one sense, *The Fountains of Paradise* (1978) is about a "space elevator," a device for lifting payloads into space without rockets. The book describes a set of four incredibly strong and thin "tapes" which stretch from the surface of the planet to a satellite in a synchronous orbit. Up those tapes will eventually be built a "huge, fluted column," a fountain (at least in shape), the spurt of which does not fall back to Earth but continues to rise into space. The fountainlike column is also a "bridge to the stars."

More important, the book is about the designer of this "ultimate bridge," Vannevar Morgan, a man driven by the desire to be famous. He has already built a bridge across the Strait of Gibraltar; now he wants to build a tower that will make him as famous as Gustave Eiffel. He is a man who has fought the good fight against the forces of Nature almost since the day when he, then a small boy, lost a kite to the wind. He later learned, not only to control his kites, but also how to run up their strings little squares of cardboard with his name on them, squares which he then twitched free on small parachutes. He always hoped someone would find one of the little squares and send it back to him. It is very much to the novel's point that no one ever did. And that the Gibraltar Bridge is not named after him.

The tone of the book is valedictory. All of the major characters are in their later years. A television reporter, a sort of Barbara Walters who used to force her way to every story, finds that she no longer wants to push as hard as she once did. A retired diplomat, a man who has had his fill of power, finds that he no longer envies, as apparently he once did, the relative immortality of his computer; he is content to leave the world to those who will come after him. Even Vannevar Morgan, who is not the sort of man ever likely to slow down, who dies of a heart attack in the book's penultimate scene, is able to believe before his death that his work has been worthwhile even if he is not remembered for it. He is able to see the space elevator as his gift to the race, and that is probably as close as he could ever get to the diplomat's willingness to pass and be forgotten with the rest.

Morgan's last act, the act that brings on his heart attack, is to take a construction vehicle up the tapes to rescue some people stranded at a way station. That act, that saving, as we learn from the novel's final chapter, is appropriate. Fifteen hundred years after Morgan's death, not only is his tower still standing, but it has allowed the human race to escape from an Earth which is passing into a new ice age. People have escaped, some to the inner planets, but most to a "ring city" which circles the globe. Morgan's tower has managed to save the whole race.

That some such future, some such ring city, may be the direction of destiny occurs to Morgan during his last ride up the tapes. He knows that the rings of Saturn, Uranus, and Neptune are probably not the sign of life, but it nonetheless pleases him to imagine that such rings might be "the shattered fragments" of such cities. He is able to picture a "wheel" of space stations around the Earth, all of them fed by towers such as his.

Morgan's own sense that there may be such a thing as destiny has been growing during this, his last, project. He had to displace a Buddhist monastery to get a proper base for his tower. The monks, not surprisingly, did not want to move; but when one of them, a meteorologist of great reputation who had retired from the world, tried to destroy Morgan's first efforts with an arranged hurricane (such weather control has been for a long time possible), the plan backfired: the winds forced flights of butterflies to the top of the mountain, thus fulfilling an ancient prophecy which says that the monks have to leave. Morgan had resented the feeling of "being moved by forces beyond his understanding"; but the fact of this near-miracle, the realization that he lives in "a universe where a few dead butterflies can balance a billion-ton tower," forces him to conclude that the gods, "whatever gods" there "may be," must be on his side. He is able to entrust himself and his project to the flow of events, at least as much as any such man is ever able so to entrust.

The question of whether there are gods is another way of coming to the same point. Some years before Morgan begins his tower, there passes through the solar system a robot space probe from another star. One of the things the probe announces is that of all the cultures it has visited only those with a two-parent reproductive system and an extended childhood engage in "religious activities." The "hypothesis" known as God, the probe goes on, seems an unnecessary doubling of the problem of understanding the cosmos. If one tries to understand a god as well as the universe, then one has gone beyond, without any gain in information, that which can be investigated.

What is clear, the probe reports, is that there is a direction to evolution. The probe names five levels of culture and hints at more. What the novel would argue, as would all of Clarke's fiction, is that those levels are reason enough to trust the human desire to reach for the stars.

And besides, and this is the novel's main theme, all of the race's endeavors can be seen as examples of just such reaching. The story of Morgan and his ultimate bridge is prefaced and compared to the story of Kalidasa, a first-century Sinhalese king who built the "fountains of paradise" referred to in the title (the whole novel is set on the island of Taprobane, which does not exist but which is imagined as being "about ninety percent congruent" with Sri Lanka). Kalidasa's efforts to establish some "claim to divinity," at least to the immortality of fame, are embodied in the beautiful gardens and fountains at the base of a butte and in the palace at the top. He calls the former Paradise and the latter Heaven, but the novel is more interested in presenting his whole desire as an anticipation of Morgan's similar motivation and engineering feat. There is something about the king's character, Morgan admits, which strikes a chord in the "secret places" of his own heart.

Kalidasa is opposed by the monks on a nearby peak, the same monks Morgan later has to have removed, because "no man should challenge the gods." But, as Morgan tries to explain in defense of his own project, such desires are not that different from the longings for perfection that brought the monks to their mountaintop. His space elevator, he says, might well be seen as just "an extension" of the stairway they have built to the top of their peak, a continuation "all the way to heaven."

The symbol of the universality of this upward striving is the "perfectly symmetrical, sharp-edged triangle," "deepest blue" in color, which the monks' peak casts upon the clouds at dawn. (For a picture of the phenomenon Clarke has in mind, see the January 1979 number of *National Geographic*, page 143.) Pilgrims climb all night to behold this "famous shadow," this symbol "for each" "to interpret" as he will. The interpretation the book gives is clear from its next-to-the-last scene, from the moment when Vannevar Morgan, just dead of a heart attack, is being carried back down his space elevator. He cannot see it, of course, but the mountain casts its upward-pointing shadow exactly as before, even though it is now the base of his ultimate bridge. The pilgrims may not visit any more, but they will be replaced by new pilgrims going to the stars.

The book's final scene is set fifteen hundred years in the future, after the senders of the space probe have finally arrived. The Starholmer, as humans call "It," is especially interested in humanity's children. Since It is not Itself a being who either matures or dies, It hopes to better understand adult humans by understanding those who have not yet either matured or come to fear death.

The Starholmer's most difficult problem, however, is trying to understand why humans see fantasy as a kind of fact. It sees fantasy as, if anything, the opposite of fact. But humans, the whole novel has insisted, have always tried to rise above their limits, have always reached for the fantastic. The still-standing space elevator, now called Kalidasa's Tower even though the king lived two thousand years before the now forgotten Morgan, is appropriately so named: it embodies humanity's repeated urge to take the next step in understanding the cosmos. It in fact embodies the human urge to become gods.

The Starholmer is not mortal and so knows neither "awe" nor "fear." Humans, having always been mortal, have always used fantasy to cope with both awe and fear, to escape in imagination the limits of mortality. The children the Starholmer is talking to are evolving into creatures who can deal directly with reality, who no longer need machines. Perhaps it is only cultures with two-parent reproduction and extended childhood that can evolve into that level which humans always meant when they dreamed of becoming gods.

Clarke's most recent novel, *2010: Odyssey Two* (1982), is a sequel to *2001: A Space Odyssey*. In it, Heywood Floyd, the space program administrator from the earlier book, is part of a joint Russian-American expedition to visit David Bowman's deserted ship, the *Discovery*. In the course of the story we learn that Hal can be trusted, that David Bowman still cares, and that we are all watched over—but not necessarily saved— by the gods. What we learn, in other words, is what we learn from all of Clarke's novels: that the ancient legends of the race are in some sense true.

The book does a nice job of creating an atmosphere of fear when the expedition reaches the *Discovery*. The dark corridors of the derelict, the empty spacesuits hanging helmetless, and even a specific reference to the science-fiction film *Alien* are used to introduce and underline the fear that Hal is somehow still alive and will somehow run amuck again.

It does turn out that Hal can be reconnected, that he can in that sense be brought back from the dead. And the rest of the novel does build much suspense on the fear that he cannot be trusted. The difference this time is the presence of Dr. Chandra, Hal's builder. To a certain extent, the answer to Hal's original problem is represented by the joint Russian-American mission. The divided aims of *Discovery*'s original instructions have been brought somewhat closer together by the coming together of the humans who issue those instructions. But Dr. Chandra, who, although small, is presented as being much taller morally than the rest of the crew, embodies in himself the nonviolent approach to other intelligent life which is the key to working with Hal. Chandra assumes, as a film like *Alien* does not, that any intelligent life will respond positively to the reasonableness of cooperation and nonaggression. He points out that we may all be seen as machines, some based on carbon, some on silicon, and that Hal, as another intelligent machine, is deserving of "appropriate respect." Chandra turns out, of course, to be right. Hal not only performs his duties exactly as assigned, but he is able—at a climactic moment in the story—to agree to what may well endanger his very existence. He is able to agree that it is reasonable that he risk his life for the sake of the mission, for the greater good. More than that we cannot ask of any of the carbon-based machines we feel so much closer to. The suspense about whether Hal will perform correctly, in other words, becomes more than just a worry about whether a machine will do as its designer intended; it becomes a wondering if Hal will be able—as any brave human must—to forget self in the name of duty.

The second thing we learn is that David Bowman still cares.

At the end of *2001* we were introduced to the Star-Child, told that it was such a different sort of being, so much further evolved, that we could not imagine much of what it would be or do. Even in that novel, however, we were also told that the beings who left the monoliths, who had evolved from flesh to machine to pure energy, still "had not wholly forgotten their origin in the warm slime of a vanished sea." They continue to be interested in their attempts to encourage intelligent life wherever it might seem to have a chance.

Bowman, we find out in this new novel, is more concerned even than that. He visits his dying mother, the site of his brother's untimely death, an old girlfriend, and even the inside of the *Discovery*. He may be evolving "beyond love and hate and desire and fear," but he is still—in the year 2010—more than a little susceptible to them. He not only understands how such emotions rule "the world of which he had once been a part," but he has not yet completely outgrown them.

Bowman is very much aware that he is being used as a "probe" by the beings who have changed him. For them he surveys the struggling attempts of evolution to produce intelligent life in the frozen oceans of Europa, one of Jupiter's moons, and plunges to the core of the giant planet itself. In a very poignant moment he visits on Earth Olduvai Gorge and seems to see there, inside one of those by now familiar black monoliths, the "sad and puzzled eyes" and "hairy, receding forehead" of what he does not—but we do—recognize as Moon-Watcher.

Bowman does not resent being so used, no more than do any of Clarke's other heroes who can feel themselves caught up in larger movements. It is too much of a relief to find that there are such directions to resent them when they show themselves. On the way to becoming a god, which is what is happening to him, he still takes time to comfort the mother who thought him dead, and to warn Floyd when the monolith-makers decide (borrowing from *The Sands of Mars*) to turn Jupiter into a sun (so that the chances of intelligent life evolv-

ing on Europa may be improved). He even manages to save
Hal—by having him too turned into a being of pure energy—
when the *Discovery* is destroyed by the explosion of Jupiter.
(Bowman may have a guilty conscience: his memory of dis-
mantling Hal is much clearer than his memory of Hal's killing
of Poole and the others.)

Bowman's central memory, however, the event of his life to
which he returns when he returns to Earth, is the untimely
death of his teen-age brother when he (Bowman) was only
twelve. Clarke's astronaut (Kubrick's too for that matter)
was, we know from *2001*, a man without close family ties. In
this book we learn that it was the death of his hero-worshipped
big brother that proved too momentous to recover from.
Bowman did, when older, even have an affair with his brother's former girlfriend, but that only made any relationship
which did not include the mutual longing for his dead brother
impossible. Bowman became, while still well this side of the
Star-Gate, a largely unemotional being, a creature evolved
beyond ordinary human concerns. He is not something we
envy—Floyd, who has something of the same tendency, even
pitied him when they knew each other—since we probably
would not want to be gods either. The point is that in *2010*
Bowman has not yet become the totally different being we
thought of him as being at the end of *2001*. He has evolved
farther in the direction that the fact of death—the refusal to
risk again such loss—had already forced him; but he is still
capable of caring for the race from which he sprang.

The novel's central consciousness, the former space administrator Heywood Floyd, has passed through a similar evolution. He has, in the years since 2001, lost his first wife to an
airplane crash and grown distant from his daughters. He has
remarried, a lady twenty years his junior, but it is more a
marriage of "contentment" than "happiness," and he is unable
to escape the "occasional depressions" and constant "wistful
sadness" that this is a world in which we must lose our loved
ones. His new marriage has given him a son, whom he dearly

loves, but Floyd is basically the kind of mature man—one who has outgrown the emotional obsessions of youth—whom Clarke has found congenial in several books (*Childhood's End*, most notably, but also *The Sands of Mars* and *The Fountains of Paradise*). Such a central character allows a concentration on larger issues, an escape from the demands of a love story. (Floyd reminds me of Walter Cronkite.)

When his new wife makes up her mind to divorce him, having decided that his willingness to go on the Jupiter mission is a failure of love for her, Floyd does suffer. But his suffering is mitigated—more quickly than it might be in the case of a younger man—by the knowledge he gains on the mission.

The importance of this detachment in the story, this focus beyond human relationships, is probably not properly appreciated unless it is juxtaposed to the moment when the very primitive life form on Europa destroys both a part of itself and a Chinese spaceship when it follows its instinct to reach for the light. The way we are supposed to view such a tragedy is made clear by a discussion aboard the Russian-American ship. When one of the crew members suggests that no animal with "elementary powers of reasoning" allows itself to be such a "victim of instinct," another replies that "one of the brightest engineers in my class was fatally attracted to a blonde in Kiev." The line is something of a joke, of course, but it also echoes the suggestion that the natural process of maturity—and perhaps of evolution—is away from such fatal attractions.

Human love becomes in this book, in fact, a matter of exchanging "vulnerabilities," an embracing in the face of death. When the Russian-American ship is rounding Jupiter in order to use its atmosphere to brake, one of the young Russian women seeks out Floyd's couch. She is not seeking sex, but solace during the dangerous moments when the ship may overheat and collapse. After the rounding is successfully completed, she falls asleep in his arms; and Floyd himself is aware of an "almost postorgasmic drowsiness." The relationship was entirely chaste, but the two afterward "know a special tenderness toward each other."

This concentration—obsession almost—with death is given a wider focus by what Dave Bowman, in his new incarnation, finds on Europa. Deep in that moon's frozen seas he discovers that rivers of lava, forced from its core by the gravity of nearby Jupiter, have made paths of warmth. More than that, he finds along the banks of these rivers evidence that "species after species" has "evolved and flourished and passed away." Europa is a planet of underice oases, all of them completely isolated from each other, places where "whole cultures and even civilizations" might rise and fall and never be aware of each other. It is a planet where intelligent life could evolve, but where the sources of such life, the climate it needs, are so "sporadic and constantly shifting" that it will have no more chance than do the man-apes at the opening of *2001*. The whole world, for that matter, is doomed to be lifeless: the tidal forces that create the warm rivers are "steadily weakening." Soon it will be a planet of ice.

The answer to such a doom, in this book as in its predecessor, is interference on the part of the monolith-makers. The book repeats from *2001* (and from "The Sentinel") the description of those who came to our solar system so long ago. "They saw how often the first faint sparks of intelligence flickered and died in the cosmic night." They had found, wherever they looked, "nothing more precious than Mind," and so "they encouraged its dawning everywhere." In this book, however, there is rather more awareness of the fact that sometimes these "farmers in the fields of stars" "had to weed." In *2001* there is no remarking on the fact that other species may have to die as Moon-Watcher's children inherit the Earth. In *2010* there is an acknowledgment that there is life on Jupiter (the life Howard Falcon found there), life which is destroyed when the giant planet is made into a sun to warm Europa. There is the admission that the choice of Europa over Jupiter was just that: a choice. Jupiter seemed an evolutionary dead-end; Europa much more likely to produce intelligent life.

The new star, then, is appropriately named. It is called "Lucifer" and is acknowledged to have "brought evil as well as good." The name also means "Light-bringer," and the book clearly feels, as its Epilog (set in 20,001) argues, that in this case the monolith-makers were right: Europa has developed intelligent life. The book is very like both Wells' and Clarke's stories called "The Star" in that the new star, like the Star of Bethlehem, heralds a new view of the universe. The views are not the same: Wells' star announces a random universe, Clarke's Jesuit's a universe that is still beautiful even without a human-centered divine plan, and "Lucifer" a universe where intelligence is in a constant—and seemingly successful— struggle to develop manifestations of itself. The last, which is almost Manichean in its division of the universe into the forces of light and dark, clearly seems to Clarke closer to the facts of human experience than does a view that sees the universe as either purely random or dominated by an omnipotent creator. It is a universe in which even the gods have evolved, and it is bound to seem attractive to those of us who have lived after Darwin, who are aware of how fragile both life and intelligence seem, who would welcome such a new star even if it proclaims, as the last line of the Epilog suggests it might, a race which might replace us. At least some intelligence would inherit the solar system.

Heywood Floyd is not aware of all of this. He is aware that David Bowman in some sense still exists: Bowman speaks to him through Hal, warns him of the coming explosion of Jupiter. Floyd is aware that it is a universe in which the forces that Bowman represents do not overly interfere: the expedition is warned of Jupiter's coming explosion, but they have to figure out a way to save themselves. It is "survival of the fittest," "Darwinian selection." "If we hadn't [saved ourselves]," the ship's captain concludes, "we wouldn't have been worth saving." But Floyd is mostly aware that he no longer feels "ignored." The time when he had felt most depressed, when he wondered most whether he had sacrificed the love of his wife for nothing, when he—and all the crew, for that matter—had been closest to despair, was all the days that they floated there, next to the great monolith that Bowman had found, and entered, nine years before. The surface of the thing remains, as far as they can tell, "a blank, impenetrable wall of total darkness." After the warning from Bowman, however, and after the warning directed (through Hal) to Earth to leave Europa alone, neither Floyd nor the race he stands for can continue to feel ignored. The crew had called the monolith Zagadka— enigma; but they also called it "Big Brother," and that, as things do in Clarke, has become more appropriate than they knew at the time. The name Big Brother and all of the associations it brings from *Nineteen Eighty-four* seem consciously reacted against. No one wants a Big Brother such as Orwell imagines, but we would—Clarke clearly assumes—be glad of a Big Brother's protection and concern in this dark universe.

At any rate, it is with such knowledge, it is assured of such watching, that Floyd falls asleep at the end of the novel. He is in the slow sleep of hibernation, and he smiles throughout the long voyage home.

One might use that smile, as a matter of fact, to sum up the book. Floyd is—on the level of plot—smiling because the last thing he thinks about before he drops off is a joke. More profoundly, one might wonder whether he is smiling because he looks forward to being with his son, a sort of minor immortality in this universe of death. If so, then he may be doomed to a certain disappointment. The book is not very hopeful about children as a solace against the grave. When the returned David Bowman, somewhat desperate that something remain of his dead brother, asks the girlfriend they shared whether her son is his (David's, and therefore at best only like his brother), she lies when she answers yes. And Floyd's own son may well have a better relationship with his mother (and with the dolphins he, like other Clarke children, plays with) than he does with his long-absent father. Only Dr. Chandra, who is already working on Hal 10,000, of all the "fathers" in the book, seems likely to live on in his child.

If Floyd is thinking that the resurrection of Hal and the return of Bowman may offer some as yet undefined hope for us all, he is again probably going to be disappointed. Nothing in this second odyssey offers much help in this universe where we individuals must die. We may, as we get older, learn to identify with larger issues, with the search for truth or the preservation of the species; but we still must die. We can only hope, and that in the most general way, that the creatures into which our children evolve will continue to remember us, not specifically as Bowman remembers his mother and brother, but as we remember Moon-Watcher, as one of those who had to be so that we could be.

But if Floyd is smiling because he trusts; if he can put himself into hibernation as he and the whole ship twice, while rounding Jupiter, put themselves into the hands of the laws of celestial mechanics; if he can be at peace even though he is, as he once was while canoeing down the Colorado River, "in the grip of irresistible forces"; if he can, in his own life, both treasure and look beyond the individual, see as the "gods" have learned to do; if he can find comfort in the fact that such "gods" only interfere in this universe as he interferes in the lives of his friends—with the best of intentions—then his smile is well earned and justified.

That *2010* ends with Floyd in the near-death of hibernation is a reminder of how many of Clarke's stories are about an individual brought face to face with the fact that he really is going to die. Sometimes it does not happen: the fate is escaped for a while through unforeseen circumstances ("Summertime on Icarus," 1960, or "Maelstrom II," 1962) or through hidden resources within the individual himself ("Into the Comet," 1960). But often enough the threat is final, and the character has to come to terms with it. He does so by identifying with the larger flow, with a hope of a future for the race and perhaps even meaning in the universe. In "Death and the Senator" (1961) an ambitious man, a would-be presidential candidate, who is told that he has but six months to live, finds that he is able to forget himself in thinking of others; he gives up his ambition, regains the love of his grandchildren, and even allows younger people to take advantage of the limited availability of a treatment that might cure him. In "Transit of Earth" (1971) a scientist, on Mars to observe the transit of Earth and the Moon across the face of the Sun, is able to cope with the certainty of his own death by identifying with the knowledge he came to collect, with the colleagues who gave up their lives that he might do so, with Captain Cook, who went to the South Seas to witness a similar transit of Venus, and with Commander Scott's similarly ill-fated expedition to the South Pole. He imagines Scott's body moving slowly to the sea and his own elements being absorbed by Mars. He even re-states the human hope of meaning in the universe: he goes out playing a recording of J. S. Bach, suggesting that it may have some relationship to the almost artificial line-up of the planets he has come to record.

Early in his career, Clarke wrote a few stories in which the truth about the universe seems to be dark. The dark is all-pervasive in "The Wall of Darkness" (1949); it turns back on itself like a Möbius strip. The final truth in "A Walk in the Dark" (1950) is the "rattle of monstrous claws in the darkness *ahead*" of the protagonist. But in most of his fiction Clarke has continued to hope that, just as the legends the Europans (in *2010*) tell themselves about the birth of their sun are truer than they know, so too there is some truth to the fact that humans have peopled the sky with gods. He has continued to hope that there may be some as yet undiscovered truth embodied in his own legend about Dave Bowman, face to face with the dark wall of the monolith and able to cry: "My God, it's full of stars!"

Addendum: *The Songs of Distant Earth*

In the three years since this book first appeared, the work of Arthur C. Clarke has twice been brought before the public. In 1984 Peter Hyams released his film version of *2010*, and in 1986 Clarke himself published a new novel, *The Songs of Distant Earth*. The plan of this Addendum is to use a discussion of that film, and of a 1957 short story also called "The Songs of Distant Earth," to place this latest novel in the Clarke canon.

I

When Peter Hyams came to make the film version of *2010*, he chose to emphasize one of the novel's minor and less controversial themes. Against the background of a threatened nuclear war, and the constantly repeated hope that there will be an Earth to return to, he has the joint Russian-American expedition voyage to Jupiter, board the derelict *Discovery*, reactivate HAL, and escape the explosion of Jupiter into a new sun. What he does not have, although he has the incidents take place, is any very real sympathy for the story of David Bowman, the astronaut who, in *2001*, became a part of, a child of, the godlike forces who protect intelligent species wherever in the universe they find them.

The film opens with two scientists, a Russian and an American, agreeing to persuade their governments to launch the joint venture. It continues with the two crews gradually warming to each other, learning each other's languages and saving each other's lives. It makes emblematic moments by focusing on things such as the shoulder patches of two of the astronauts, a man and a woman, one from each crew, as they embrace during a particularly frightening part of the voyage. And it ends by adding to the message Clarke has the forces behind the monoliths deliver, that humans are not to interfere with the life that is developing on Europa, the much more historically specific instructions that humans are welcome to use the rest of the worlds of the solar system "together" and "in peace."

This tight focus on escaping the evils of the Cold War does not give Hyams room to do much else. Instead, he falls back, as Clarke has long since quit doing, on some of the more limiting commonplaces of American adventure movies. The film's Russians, for all of the emphasis on the crews' working together, are presented as being more soft-headed than smart. It is the American scientist, the same Heywood Floyd who sent the *Discovery* out on its original mission, who, by strength of personality, is really in charge, not—as in the book—the woman who commands both the ship and the Russians. And when the film's Floyd, unlike the Floyd of the novel, finishes his mission, he knows that his young wife and son will be awaiting his return to Earth. They understood when he told them that he had to make the two-and-a-half year voyage, that he had "lost some good men" out there. The Floyd of the novel, on the other hand, hears in the midst of the trip's many crises that his young wife is going to divorce him, and he is not at all certain that, if he manages to return, he will be able to have any sort of relationship with the son from whom he has been away for so long.

Clarke's Floyd, in sum, experiences loss as well as adventure, loneliness as well as escape, and as a result is able—in a way the cardboard hero of the film never could—to find some real if limited comfort in the fact that David Bowman still exists, that the universe has not always evidenced only unconcern.

But the thing one really becomes aware of in watching Hyams' *2010* is how pointlessly borrowed much of its imagery seems. There is, for example, an early and too-long scene in which two government officials are sitting on a park bench in front of the White House. They talk about telling lies as a matter of political policy, and the result is clearly, though not particularly cleverly, intended to evoke *Doonesbury*. The discussion, however, is simply not extreme enough to justify such an appeal to other examples of high-level insanity.

Nor does there seem to be much of a reason for most of the film to have been shot, as it was, under red lights. The effect is too much like those moments of "silent running" in submarine movies. There are even times when the ribs of the ship are heard to moan and groan, as do those of submarines under attack in such films. It is as if Hyams could not think of anything else to do with a film, most of whose action takes place within the cramped quarters of a spaceship. The film's longest scene, for that matter, a spacesuited crossing from the Russian ship to the derelict *Discovery*, makes such over-use of breathing on the sound track that we feel momentarily trapped in a movie about deep-sea diving.

Even the visual references to *2001* are almost perfunctory. When the astronauts re-enter the *Discovery*, they are seen, briefly and in a very poor light, walking at those same impossible angles Kubrick went to such expense to create. When one of the Russians is about to find, as did David Bowman in the former film, that the monolith is "full of stars," we see his helmeted head with multi-colored lights reflected in its face-plate, a simple copying of one of *2001*'s frequently reproduced scenes. And when the expert who designed HAL reconnects that computer, the scene is an uninspired and even long-winded reverse of the scene in *2001* in which Bowman, floating in the red-lighted interior of HAL's brain, disconnects the insane computer. Hyams has HAL gradually regain sophistication, but really only up to the point of being ready to ask again for a first lesson. There is none of the intensity that HAL's reversion to singing "Daisy, Daisy" created in the earlier film.

The truth of the matter is, I think, that Hyams just did not have any very close identification with anything Clarke had to say. I have argued in a previous chapter that *2001* the film and *2001* the novel are very different things, but they have a relationship of sympathy that is seldom present in this filming of a Clarke novel.

Take the matter of HAL, for example. Although the film tries to make us care when the expert who created HAL brings the computer back to life, we don't. And the problem is that Hyams himself has no respect for the machine, no sense of its near-humanity. What the film offers us is not a personality but a talking camera lens. HAL is presented as being about as sophisticated (and as nagging) as the buzzer that insists one buckle one's seat belt; no more than that.

As a result, when the expedition has to use the *Discovery* to launch the Russian ship, an action that is sure to end in the destruction of both the *Discovery* and HAL, the suspense as to whether the computer will perform as ordered does not really occur. Waiting to see if HAL will malfunction again is about as suspenseful as waiting to see if a car will start on a cold morning. The HAL of this film does not really come alive until it (not he) is addressed by the ghost (or whatever it is) of Dave Bowman. Then the machine, recognizing its true master's voice, manages to say with real enthusiasm that it is "so good to be working with you again, Dave." Hyams, to put it another way, returns the uppity HAL to its place; it is not reborn, it is just plugged in again.

Hyams does have David Bowman return and warn the expedition that it must leave, but the whole appearance of this representative of the forces behind the monoliths has about it a certain distance, a sense of remove, that demonstrates that Hyams was not interested in what might be called the supernatural aspects of the novel. When David Bowman appears, on Earth, to his former wife, he does so by imposing himself on the TV picture she is watching. He says that he includes all that really was Dave Bowman, but that is exactly the point: it is all as if he is recorded. When Floyd follows Bowman's single appearance through the corridors of the *Discovery*, he sees him as a young man in an orange spacesuit, as a white-haired man dressed in black, as an old man in a white gown, and as the foetus of whatever he has become—images which are taken directly from *2001*. The feeling given by the film is not that of seeing reality created on the screen; it is the feeling of watching a filmmaker watch a film, one he did not particularly want to see.

Clarke's *2010*, as I have said elsewhere in this book, embodies the hope that, just as the legends the Europans of the far distant future tell themselves about the birth of their sun are truer than they can know, so too there is some as yet undiscovered truth to the fact that humans have always peopled their sky with gods. Hyams' film, on the other hand, is not interested in anything beyond the expedition's escape from the blow-up of Jupiter and, by extension, of Earth itself in a nuclear war. The film's characters say "My God" a lot, but the film itself does not care about gods at all.

II

Remembering, if only by contrast, the supernatural center of Clarke's *2010* gives a context for discussing his latest novel, *The Songs of Distant Earth*, and especially how it is not only a rewriting and expansion of a short story he published thirty years ago, but also a re-asking of the question that is raised in that story, the question that novels such as *Childhood's End, 2001,* and *2010* were meant to answer affirmatively: is the hope that there may be meaning in the universe sufficient to comfort the individual against the certainty of mortality?

The short story, "The Songs of Distant Earth," was published in 1957. It is set on a planet a hundred light-years from Earth, a planet more than nine-tenths water and thus appropriately named Thalassa, the Latinized form of the Greek word for sea (another echo of Clarke's boyhood reading of Swinburne, in this case of the poem "Thalassius").

Thalassa is described as having an island culture that has, in the three hundred years since the planet was settled by men and women from Earth, regressed to something resembling those 1940s movies starring people such as Dorothy Lamour and Jon Hall and set somewhere south of Pago Pago. Clarke's story opens, as such films always do, with a beach, palm trees, a teasing maiden, and a handsome young fisherman standing there with "one hand twined around the rigging" of his ocean-going canoe.

This "simple, carefree world" is invaded, not by the sails of a European ship, but by that most 1950-ish of sights and sounds, a "vapor trail" drawn as if by "a piece of chalk across the blue vault of heaven," "the thin scream" of an aircraft descending, as were all those experimental planes after World War II, "from the borders of space." This island world is interrupted, to put it another way, by that most 1950-ish of movie scenes: the landing of a visiting spaceship. The first part of this story climaxes, as does the first part of Clarke's 1953 novel, *Childhood's End*, with the opening door of a landed spaceship.

What step out, however, are not the monsters of the films, not even the mysterious devil figures of *Childhood's End*. What step out are instead just ordinary human beings, visitors from Earth. They are in fact, to continue the 50s reference, and as the rest of the story makes clear, something very like invaders in grey flannel suits.

The story is not, then, a science fiction version of *Mutiny on the Bounty*. It does not open with Fletcher Christian seeing the saronged island women. Instead, it opens with some harassed engineers, whose ship has been in serious danger, making a fortunate planet-fall on a world made up mostly of water, the very thing they need to repair the ice shield their ship pushes ahead of itself as it travels near the speed of light. The story opens with one of the young engineers seeing one of Thalassa's maidens, but his reaction reminds the reader more of the tired businessman getting off the commuter train than of anything else. He is always seen hurrying about the village "with a bulging briefcase," and when he first sees the maiden: "The anxious furrows faded from [his] brow, the tense lines slowly relaxed; and presently he smiled."

The young woman so seen, for that matter, is an island princess only in the most 1950-ish of fashions. She works as a secretary in the office of her father, the village mayor, an employment that suggests that she does not have to work for a living, that she is just marking time until she and her local boyfriend get married.

The story is, then, the product of its decade as well as of its author. Its characters owe as much to the films and fiction represented by Sloan Wilson as its plot does to the debased versions of Nordhoff and Hall. But the truth of those debts should not be allowed to obscure what becomes equally clear as the story progresses, that Clarke meant to use the love between a spaceship officer and an island maiden, a love that most of his readers would recognize as probably doomed, to represent nothing less than the insufficiency of human affection when it is seen against the immensity of the universe (as Thalassa's little islands are seen against the planet's single giant ocean).

When the lovers are first alone together, they stare "at each other across the wrinkled sand [of one of those wave-marked beaches Clarke uses so often], each wondering at the miracle that had brought them together out of the immensity of time and space."

Before the meeting, the spaceman had been looking up into the nighttime sky of this new planet and had recognized "mighty Rigel, no fainter for all the added light years its rays must now cross before they reached his eyes." He also recognized what "must be giant Canopus, almost in line with their destination, but so much more remote that even when they reached their new home, it would seem no brighter than in the skies of Earth." Before such sights he shakes his head, "as if to clear the stupefying, hypnotic image of immensity from his mind."

The young woman, in turn, having realized that the "lives" of people, "all their hopes and fears," are "so little" when seen against the "inconceivable immensities" that the space travelers have "dared to challenge," finds that the "cold of space" freezes her heart, that she, product of a 1950s imagination as she is, longs "for her home and family," for the "little room" that holds everything she owns and is "all the world" she knows or wants.

It is in this context that "the songs of distant Earth" are to be heard. The Thalassans are treated, about half-way through the story, to a recorded concert of some of the music that has been composed on Earth during the hundreds of years since their ancestors left that planet. They hear of "things" that belong "to Earth, and to Earth alone. The slow beat of mighty bells, climbing like invisible smoke from old cathedral spires; . . . the merged murmur of ten million voices as man's greatest cities woke to meet the dawn; . . . the roar of mighty engines climbing upward on the highway to the stars."

But the most important motif in the songs is hardly peculiar to Earth. "A clear soprano voice" sings "a dirge for all loves lost in the loneliness of space," a song that speaks "as clearly" to those who are "sundered from Earth by a dozen generations" as it does to those who, awakened from "suspended animation" by the threat to their ship, think of the home planet as "only weeks away."

The dominant theme of all the songs is the loneliness that must result because humans, in the face of an immense and finally deadly universe, can only embrace each other, can only cling to other changeable and mortal selves. The lovers in the story, like "wayfarers lost in a hostile wilderness," seek "warmth and comfort beside the fire of love." "While that fire burned," the story goes on to say, "they were safe from the shadows that prowled the night; and all of the universe of stars and planets shrank to a toy that they could hold within their hands."

The half-echo from Marvell's urging of the coy mistress, if that is what it is, is in service of the much more Swinburnian certainty that love must die. It is inevitable, in a story as obsessed as this one is with the unimportance of individual humans in an immense universe, that the illusion of control will end and the lovers separate. Clarke's lovers are not star-crossed; they are typical.

The story does argue, as science fiction of the fifties often does, that humans have another kind of control, an important one, though not yet up to the illusion the lovers have in each other's arms. The engineers from Earth are able to lift "about a million tons of water" from the surface of the planet to the edge of space, where it is fashioned into a shield to protect the starship from the bits of "cosmic junk" it encounters as it races on at speeds near that of light.

The lifting of the water is seen by the island maiden as being a godlike accomplishment. "It was as if . . . an invisible finger had reached down from the sky and was stirring the sea." But, as the story is at pains to point out, it is really just a feat of engineering. The waves, which had seemed to be building up into a small storm, are seen to be "marching in step, more and more swiftly in a tight circle." The resulting waterspout becomes a "spinning tower of water" that pierces the clouds "like an arrow" and heads "towards space." The engineers, who had been seen as "a tiny group of figures silhouetted against the ocean, staring out to sea," become "the little band of men who had summoned this monster from the deep, and who still stood watching it with calm assurance, ignoring the waves that were breaking almost against their feet." The accomplishment is, as such things always are in Clarke, a matter of "balance," the control of "immense and invisible forces" through knowledge, not brute strength; but the control is there. If humans are not yet able to make of the universe a toy, they may be someday. When the ship, for example, is finally ready to leave Thalassa, its propulsion system is described, again as such systems almost always are in Clarke, as using nothing less than the fires that power the "suns themselves."

And it is certainly in pursuit of such control that the spaceman decides to leave the island planet. When the engineers have finished their task, he, like Aeneas at a similar moment, seeing the expression on the maiden's face, stops celebrating and somewhat shamefacedly, "almost like a schoolboy caught in some crime," admits that the ship will be leaving soon.

What the story continues to focus on, however, is not how humans may one day be able—as in *2010*—to turn a Jupiter into a sun, but how the spaceman, creation of the fifties as he is, is inevitably going to be unable to find the embrace of the maiden sufficient. The dialogue is more that of a Western fil· of the fifties than of a South Sea Island film of the forties, but the outcome is just as predictable: "You can't leave," she says. "Stay here on Thalassa!" "I could never be happy here, where there aren't any more frontiers," he replies. "In a month I should die of boredom." Like the loner of the Western film, the spaceship officer is really married to the always hopeful possibilities of the future.

Having said all that, however, we still have not gotten at the center of this story. For at the finish of what has seemed a fairly routine piece of 1950s science fiction, a contrast between a part of the human race that is going into space and a part that is going to stay on the planet, the author, who has throughout given every sign of having favored the adventuresome, suddenly asks in the story's last line, of the future of these seemingly very different types of people, those who will voyage to the stars and those who will not: "And which was better, who could say?" In the context of the story this concluding question comes as a complete surprise, even a *non sequitur.*

But it is, as much current criticism has taught us, in such moments, through such disjunctures that texts reveal the divided motives that produce them. In this case the attempt to understand how such a question might have at any time seemed the appropriate ending to the story is a way of understanding the question behind the question, the question behind the standard stories this story tries to use to celebrate humanity's mission to conquer the universe.

And it is true that much of the story's last scene seems to say more than it had intended to say. It really is as if some undeniable other meaning insists on declaring itself.

When the island maiden watches the departure of the spaceship, she does so from the arms of the young fisherman we saw her with in the story's first scene. "This was where she belonged," we are told; "her heart would not stray again." At the same time, however, instead of being told that the "comfort" she takes in the embrace is the comfort of old love restored, we are told that it is "comfort against the loneliness of space." What she finds in the arms of the fisherman, in other words, is exactly what she found in the arms of the more romantic-seeming spaceman. Against something as general as "the loneliness of space," this story cannot keep from admitting, all embraces are alike, all lovers the same.

Similarly, when the story tells us that the young fisherman knows that "all the days of his life" the "ghost" of the spaceman will come between him and his beloved, it cannot refrain from also telling us that the ghost is the ghost of a man who will be, because he will spend the next two hundred years or so in deep hibernation, "not a day older" when they have been long "in their graves." The ghost, in other words, in spite of what the story sets out to say, is less the ghost of a former lover than it is the fact of someone still alive, of other generations, of other people who will be living when we are dead. It is not just the immensity of space against which humans ineffectively embrace, it is the certainty of death.

And so, although the story wants to have the maiden realize that while "her descendants eight generations hence [will] still be dreaming beneath the sun-soaked palms," the spaceman "and his companions [will] be moving seas, leveling mountains, and conquering unknown perils," the very next line, the last line of the story, asks: "And which was better, who could say?" For the truth that the story wants to suppress but cannot is that there is no difference. Eight or eighteen generations hence the spaceman's descendants will also be embracing against the cold of space, will also be loving and having children against the fall of night. The story's last line, in brief, is so honest that, upon reflection, it runs a thread of doubt back through the general direction of this story of the sailor-engineer-Western hero, who, having a job that he must do, has got to be traveling on. It may well be, this story almost says in spite of itself, that such a sense of direction, such a claim that the existence of the species has meaning, such a hope really of some kind of immortality, is finally as insufficient as is the embrace of another mortal to comfort the individual against the certainty of the grave.

So bright is that thread of doubt, for that matter, that following it back through the work leads one to see a part of the story's first line in a very different way. There the island maiden, who has been watching for the arrival of her fisherman's boat, sees it finally as "a tiny notch on the horizon—the only flaw in the perfect mating of the sea and sky." Given the doubt induced by the story's last line, the reader cannot but wonder if humanity's urge to find meaning or comfort is not simply a "flaw," an aberration, if you will, in the perfection of an inhuman and uncaring universe. Or, as another writer of Clarke's generation, Albert Camus, would have put it (and with the same hope that the answer is not an easy one): is it not absurd that a mortal creature should have such yearnings for immortality?

III

When, twenty-two years later, in 1979, Clarke rewrote "The Songs of Distant Earth" as a movie outline, he changed some parts of the story, but, by and large, it still remains the same: it still asks, in spite of itself, whether humans can find any comfort, as the title of his first novel puts it, *Against the Fall of Night*.

The biggest change in the movie outline is that the sun—our sun—has exploded, become a supernova. As a result the visiting ship, which was one of the last to escape, no longer has a home. Earth is no longer just distant; it is non-existent. And as a result of that, the visitors from space, instead of looking forward to further traveling, much envy the people on the island planet their Earth-type world, which in this version is called Oceana.

The people of Oceana, in turn, are made to feel "a little guilty about their past indolence" by the arrival of these star-travelers. There is this time, however, some potential for change in the island life, for something other than lying under the palm trees for generation after generation. Beneath the sea of the planet in this version of the story another life form is evolving, a species that may well challenge humans for the "future of the planet." This "threat from the deep," we are told, "may be exactly what is needed to revitalize" the people of Oceana.

The direction this retelling of the story wants to go, then, is fairly clear. The visitors from space are not only to repair their shield, but also to assist the local people in their first contact with alien beings. The technological prowess of the visitors is to act as a stimulus to the island culture, helping it to prepare itself to meet the future challenge it will face, not in the depths of space, but on Oceana itself.

Drawing upon his experience with Kubrick, Clarke sketches in how the film is to present both the developing species and the examples of human prowess that are to counter it. The under-ocean beings are described as "giant squidlike creatures, which communicate in the total darkness of the abyss by beautiful displays of multi-colored luminescence." The counter-force, the sort of technology that is to inspire the island people, is represented by the "slow-motion ice ballet" of the shield-building and by the ignition, "brighter than 100 suns," of the departing ship.

There is another scene, however, that Clarke cannot keep from describing. In it are the "spectacular views of the destruction of the solar system, recorded by cameras on Earth and some other planets: Jupiter boiling, Saturn's rings collapsing, the sun finally devouring its children, but, most poignant of all, unbearably moving scenes of the last moments of beloved earthscapes and artifacts (*e.g.*, the Taj Mahal, St. Peter's, the Pyramids, etc., melting down)." And it is difficult to see how such moments, filmed as here presented, would not so dominate the action as to make the rest of the movie seem irrelevant.

Which is exactly the point. This story is finally no more under Clarke's complete control than was its earlier version. In this one, as in the other, humans will travel on to a far distant planet only to find there, as they could have found on Oceana and as their ancestors found on Earth, the challenge that produces technological progress. While such progress may be beautiful and certainly seems necessary, especially in a universe of giant squidlike competitors and suns that explode, the story's very lack of any strong sense of direction is an admission that telling about more and more technological progress on more and more planets, about fighting the same battle for existence over and over again, is just another rendering of the tale about the bear who went over the mountain to see what he could see, and found there that the other side looked very much like the side he had just left.

All of which brings us back to the central question. If it makes no difference whether one stays on Oceana or voyages to an Earth-type planet somewhere else, if identification with one's race's mission is just identification with a replay of the evolutionary struggle, then is there any other comfort against the certainty that plagued the lovers at the end of the first version of "The Songs of Distant Earth," the certainty that this is a universe in which both planets and people die? The only possibilities this movie outline has to offer are the moment when the spaceman "plugs in temporarily to the recorded skills and personality of a long-dead deep-sea explorer" in order to investigate the giant squidlike creatures, and the fact that "the golden

mask of the young Pharaoh Tutankhamun [*sic*], one of the last
treasures saved from Earth," stands at the door of the "hibernaculum" in the spaceship, guarding "the sleeping as once it
guarded the dead." And neither of these false immortalities, the
recording of the dead man or the possibility of reawakening
those in hibernation, as the Egyptians hoped the dead could be
reawakened, is seriously offered as an answer to the outline's
last scene, a scene which is pretty much a repeat of the same
scene in the earlier story. In this, the island maiden and her
local lover, both of whom have loved the spaceman (a new
twist, that, over the 1957 story), are very aware that the child of
the spaceman the woman now carries (another twist on the
earlier story) is a "child whose father will remember them when
he awakens," but that that awakening will be—as the last line
of the outline emphasizes—"centuries after they have turned to
dust."

IV

By the time, a half-dozen or so years later, Clarke had finished the novel-length version of *The Songs of Distant Earth* (it
was published in 1986), he had gained more control over his
material. But this most recent book is still a good deal less optimistic than are *Childhood's End, 2001,* and *2010.* It is, for
that matter, even less optimistic than it seems to realize.

While the novel retains, from the movie outline, the destroyed Earth and the evolving new species on the new planet, it
opens with an interesting distinction between the "seedship"
that originally settled what is again called Thalassa and the
ship full of living humans that makes a planned—not accidental—stop to repair its ice-shield. Whereas the seedship carried "genotypes" out of which robots bred the whole culture of
Thalassa, the visiting ship, powered by a "quantum drive" that
works on the stuff of space itself, carries in hibernation, in addition to the crew that has been awakened to repair the shield, a
million members of Earth's last generation. The point seems to
be that the culture thus transmitted is a mature culture, capable

of much control of its destiny; it is not, as is Thalassa's still adolescent society, the result of a racial scattering of seed.

The book seems vaguely to hope that, by having Earth's culture escape the flames, it will itself escape the problem of having the ship's final mission—on the far-off planet Sagan Two—seem a simple repetition of what the Thalassans will face on their planet and that our ancestors faced in Earth's own past. But when that mission comes to be described, impressive as it is, it is still just the struggle for existence. The ship will use its quantum drive to warm and to change the orbit of that far-off planet, but even that stunning piece of engineering—a feat worthy of the forces behind the monoliths—is just a faster and more controlled version of what took millions of years in Earth's own past. Staggering as such an accomplishment will be, it does not finally answer the question that has been at the center of this story in all of its many forms. It does not tell us how to be comforted, as we stand here on this beach with our arms around our only too mortal beloved, by the vision of other members of our species doing things, however great, long after we are dead.

And so, in the novel, there are members of the ship's crew who, like Ulysses' sailors, want to cease from wandering, want to stay in the land of the Lotus-Eaters that Clarke made such use of in his earlier fiction. In this case, the people who want to stay are Martians, people who, having already seen the conquering of one cold and dangerous planet, do not want to live through such a thing again. In answer to their plea, the book offers a strong ship's captain and the argument that in the hope of survival the human race must settle as many worlds as possible. But the very strength the captain has to have (he is a man capable of torture and even murder in the name of duty) and the very fact that the argument for settling a lot of worlds is not stated more than once in the book both demonstrate that such an appeal, such an inquiry about why they should go on, has a power that cannot be answered, only ignored in the exciting description of a future application of stunning technology.

There is even a moment when *The Songs of Distant Earth* seems almost to say that the very effort to speculate about the future is doomed to failure. It happens at a party where the Thalassans and the voyagers are admiring a "gas-sculpture" called "Life," a display that encompasses "the four-billion-year odyssey from amoeba to man." When the artist tries "to go beyond," however, the work collapses into "contortions" of "fluorescent gas" that are "too complex and too abstract" to be followed. Speculations about the far future, such a moment admits, are really speculations about what is not only unknowable but in a very real sense unimaginable. All that art can do is retrace the known, positing such retracings as stretching forward into the future, perhaps to the end of the race.

But the subject the novel finally cannot get away from— any more than could the original story—is the fact that the universe is a place where individuals die. When the island maiden's younger brother and his girlfriend are examining the "incredible ribbon" that raises the ice blocks into space, what the girl hears in the sound the ribbon makes as it stretches between the surface of the planet and the orbiting ship is the sound of "the sea of space" washing "upon the shores of all its worlds—a sound terrifying in its meaningless futility as it [reverberates] through the aching emptiness of the universe." What the young man hears, on the other hand, is a sort of "Fanfare for Strings, if one could imagine such a thing," a sound that is for him, although it is "ineffably sad and distant," a "siren song." Lost in these notes, he is killed when the ice block upon which he is standing is suddenly hauled into space. The music of the spheres, one might say, turns out to be deadly.

And that death, in spite of the book's intentions to the contrary, in spite of the impressiveness of the future settlement on Sagan Two and the discovery of the evolving species that is going to invigorate life on Thalassa, becomes the true center of the novel. It is anticipated by the near-death of the spaceman in an accident (he is brought back to life by medical science), and it is the subject of reflection for the rest of the book after it happens (the boy's parents refuse to allow the space travelers to take his body away with them, for even if he could be revived in some distant future when the medical experts among the ship's passengers have been awakened, he would still have lost the world he has known). The untimely death of a young boy becomes—especially in the conversations his sister, the island maiden, has with the wise old man of the travelers—the unacknowledged subject of *The Songs of Distant Earth*.

It is not that the technological prowess of humans is ignored. The book even suggests that the quantum drive's "real purpose is nothing so trivial as the exploration of the universe." Humanity may "need its energies one day," we are told, "to stop the cosmos' collapsing back into the primordial black hole." But such speculations are dismissed finally as being about far-off unknown futures. What is knowable is that humans, whatever they can do about awakening people from the near-death of hibernation, cannot bring back the dead from their graves any more than could the Egyptians who made the mask of Tutankhamen. When the island maiden sees that mask, she does not think of immortality but of her brother who also died young. And when the spaceman brags that his people, by being able to awaken the sleepers, have learned to do what the Egyptians wanted to do, she thinks: "But not in the way I would have wished." All of which is nicely captured when, coming out of the deep cold of the hibernaculum, she touches the mask and thinks it warm, not realizing for a moment that it is only her hand still adjusting to normal temperature.

Even the discussion about God which the island maiden has with the wise old man of the space travelers is really occasioned by the death of the boy. After the old man has gone on tiresomely for most of a chapter about the difference between a personal god who notes the sparrow's fall and an impersonal god who once started the universe off, finally the maiden asks him what even he admits is "her shrewdest question": "What is the purpose of grief?" In attempting to answer that, the old man, having agreed that grief may "be an accidental—even a pathological—by-product of love," still insists that it is "our emotions that make us human," that he would not "abandon them, even knowing that each new love is yet another hostage to those twin terrorists, Time and Fate." What the book admits, in other words, is that the important question is less whether there is a God and more whether we are willing to give up caring about the death of individuals. One can imagine, the old man says, an intelligent species that would not remember the dead with emotion, that might not remember them at all. It "could be at least as successful as the termites and the ants were on Earth," but it would be, by being so uncaring, by identifying with the species and not the individual, "utterly inhuman." It would not ask, as this book asks in spite of its celebration of the future on Thalassa and Sagan Two: what does it profit the individual if the race gain the whole universe?

And so, when it comes time in the novel to play "the songs of distant Earth," the music remains sad, even though there is an effort to make it otherwise. The climax of the program is "the last great work in the symphonic tradition," a piece entitled the "Lamentation for Atlantis." In the last movement of the symphony there is a march that some have interpreted as being about "a New Atlantis emerging from the waves," but the composer is on record as having said that to him "the finale depicts the conquest of space." What is most real in the book, however, is not the end of the work but its center, the attempt to capture in music "a great city square almost as large as St. Marks or St. Peters," all around which "are half-ruined buildings, like Greek temples, and overturned statues draped with seaweeds, green fronds waving slowly back and forth." In "the center of the square" is "a low mound . . . with a pattern of lines radiating from it." After a moment, the composer concludes, he notices that the mound is "pulsing." And then that there are "two huge, unblinking eyes staring out at me." Such a vision, and the book does no more to explain it than this, whatever it may represent—sea monster, destruction, death, God—certainly remains less optimistic than the celebration of the conquest of space would try to make it.

When it comes time to do the last scene, the novel ends, as did the story and the movie outline, with the lovers on the beach aware that there will be others, including the spaceman, still living when they are "dust upon the wind." It does add, in a brilliant stroke, the fact that for years—for generations even—the ship's departing flare is still visible in the night sky. The island maiden, grown old, sees it flame up particularly brightly one night, just before her eyesight fails. And her grandchildren have no difficulty in pointing it out as a "blue, third magnitude star," now "fifteen light-away." But basically the ending is the same. Even the fact that Clarke adds a half-page epilogue set in the far future when the spaceman awakes at Sagan Two does not change anything, for the whole epilogue is about how, "when he could face the ordeal," the spaceman *would* call up from the ship's memory the pictures sent from Thalassa in the centuries since he left; he *would* see the son he left behind grow up, old, and die; and he *would* watch, because there is no way that he can avoid it, the slow aging of the long-dead girl he held in his arms what seems to him "only weeks ago." It is all to be done in the future, to happen offstage, because the book cannot bear to have it happen onstage.

The Songs of Distant Earth, in other words, repeats the question that *Childhood's End, 2001*, and *2010* were meant to answer. It would seem, as is certainly likely, that in spite of the optimism of most of his fiction, it has never been, not in 1957, 1979, or 1986, completely clear to Clarke that the discovery that our species is a part of some near-divine plan would really answer the central difficulty, that each of us will one day have to stop voyaging into the future.

Clarke's Fiction

Across the Sea of Stars
Includes *Childhood's End, Earthlight,* and eighteen stories from *Expedition to Earth, Tales from the White Hart,* and *Reach for Tomorrow.*

Against the Fall of Night

Childhood's End

The City and the Stars

The Deep Range

Dolphin Island: A Story of the People of the Sea

Earthlight

Expedition to Earth
Includes "Second Dawn," " 'If I Forget Thee, Oh Earth . . .'," "Breaking Strain," "History Lesson," "Superiority," "Exile of the Eons," "Hide and Seek," "Expedition to Earth," "Loophole," "Inheritance," and "The Sentinel."

A Fall of Moondust

The Fountains of Paradise

From the Ocean, from the Stars
Includes *The Deep Range, The Other Side of the Sky,* and *The City and the Stars.*

Forgotten Enemy," "Technical Error," "The Parasite," "The Fires Within," "The Awakening," "Trouble with the Natives," "The Curse," "Time's Arrow," "Jupiter Five," and "The Possessed."

Rendezvous with Rama

The Sands of Mars

Tales from the White Hart

Includes "Silence Please," "Big Game Hunt," "Patent Pending," "Armaments Race," "Critical Mass," "The Ultimate Melody," "The Pacifist," "The Next Tenants," "Moving Spirit," "The Man Who Ploughed the Sea," "The Reluctant Orchid," "Cold War," "What Goes Up," "Sleeping Beauty," and "The Defenestration of Ermintrude Inch."

Tales of Ten Worlds

Includes "I Remember Babylon," "Summertime on Icarus," "Out of the Cradle, Endlessly Orbiting . . . ," "Who's There?" "Hate," "Into the Comet," "An Ape about the House," "Saturn Rising," "Let There Be Light," "Death and the Senator," "Trouble with Time," "Before Eden," "A Slight Case of Sunstroke," "Dog Star," and "The Road to the Sea."

2001: A Space Odyssey

2010: Odyssey Two

The Wind from the Sun

Includes "The Food of the Gods," "Maelstrom II," "The Shining Ones," "The Wind from the Sun," "The Secret," "The Last Command," "Dial F for Frankenstein," "Reunion," "Playback," "The Light of Darkness," "The Longest Science Fiction Story Ever Told," "Herbert George Morley Roberts Wells, Esq.," "Love That Universe," "Crusade," "The Cruel Sky," "Neutron Tide," "Transit of Earth," and "A Meeting with Medusa."

Clarke's Nonfiction Mentioned in the Text

Beyond Jupiter: The Worlds of Tomorrow
The Challenge of the Spaceship: Previews of Tomorrow's World
    Includes the essays "Across the Sea of Stars" and "Of
    Space and Spirit."
"Epilogue," *First on the Moon,* by Neil Armstrong, Michael
    Collins, and Edwin E. Aldrin, Jr.
The Exploration of Space
"Introduction," *The Invisible Man* and *The War of the*
    Worlds, by H. G. Wells
The Lost Worlds of 2001
"On Moylan on *The City and the Stars,"* *Science-Fiction*
    Studies
Profiles of the Future: An Inquiry into the Limits of the Pos-
    sible
The View from Serendip
    Includes the speech "Technology and the Limits of Knowl-
    edge."

Selected Criticism

Agel, Jerome, ed. *The Making of Kubrick's* 2001. New York: New American Library, 1970.

Allen, L. David. *Science Fiction: An Introduction*. Lincoln, Nebraska: Cliff's Notes, 1973.

Ash, Brian. *Faces of the Future*. London: Elek/Pemberton, 1975.

Baxter, John. *Science Fiction in the Cinema*. New York: A. S. Barnes, 1970.

Beja, Morris. "*2001*: Odyssey to Byzantium." In Clareson's *SF: The Other Side of Realism*, pp. 263–265.

Bernstein, Jeremy. "Out of the Ego Chamber." *The New Yorker* (9 August 1969), pp. 40–65.

Boyd, David. "Mode and Meaning in *2001*." *Journal of Popular Film* 6 (1978), 202–215.

Brigg, Peter. "Three Styles of Arthur C. Clarke: The Projector, the Wit, and the Mystic." In Olander and Greenberg, pp. 15–51.

Brody, Alan. "*2001* and the Paradox of the Fortunate Fall." *Hartford Studies in Literature* 1 (1969), 7–19.

Brosnan, John. *Future Tense*. New York: St. Martin's, 1978.

Cary, Meredith. "Faustus Now." *Hartford Studies in Literature* 4 (1972), 167–173.

Chappell, Fred. "The Science Fiction Film Image: *A Trip to the Moon* to *2001: A Space Odyssey.*" In *Science Fiction Films,* ed. by Thomas R. Atkins (New York: Monarch Press, 1976), pp. 29–47.

Ciment, Michel. "The Odyssey of Stanley Kubrick: Part 3: Towards the Infinite—*2001.*" In Johnson, pp. 134–141.

Clareson, Thomas D. "The Cosmic Loneliness of Arthur C. Clarke." In Olander and Greenberg, pp. 52–71.

————, ed. *Many Futures, Many Worlds: Theme and Form in Science Fiction.* Kent, Ohio: Kent State University Press, 1977.

————, ed. *SF: The Other Side of Realism.* Bowling Green, Ohio: The Popular Press, 1971.

De Vries, Daniel. *The Films of Stanley Kubrick.* Grand Rapids, Michigan: William B. Eerdmans, 1973.

Doyno, Victor A. "*2001²:* Years and Shapes." *Hartford Studies in Literature* 1 (1969), 131–132.

Dumont, Jean-Paul, and Jean Monod. *Le Foetus Astral.* Paris: Christian Bourgois, 1970.

Eisenstein, Alex. "The Academic Overkill of *2001.*" In Clareson's *SF: The Other Side of Realism,* pp. 267–271.

Erlich, Richard D. "Strange Odyssey: From Dart and Ardrey to Kubrick and Clarke." *Extrapolation* 17 (1976), 118–124.

Fenichel, Robert R. "Comment." *Hartford Studies in Literature* 1 (1969), 133–135.

Geduld, Carolyn. *Filmguide to* 2001: A Space Odyssey. Bloomington, Indiana: Indiana University Press, 1973.

Geduld, Harry M. "Return to Méliès: Reflections of the Science Fiction Film." In Johnson, pp. 142–147.

Harfst, Betsy. "Of Myths and Polyominoes: Mythological Content in Clarke's Fiction." In Olander and Greenberg, pp. 87–120.

Hendin, Josephine. *Vulnerable People*. New York: Oxford, 1978.

Hillegas, Mark R. *The Future as Nightmare*. New York: Oxford, 1967.

Hoch, David G. "Mythic Patterns in *2001: A Space Odyssey*." *Journal of Popular Culture* 4 (1971), 961–965.

Holland, Norman N. "*2001*: A Psychosocial Explication." *Hartford Studies in Literature* 1 (1969), 20–25.

Hollow, John. "*2001* in Perspective: The Fiction of Arthur C. Clarke." *Southwest Review* 61 (1976), 113–128.

Howes, Alan B. "Expectation and Surprise in *Childhood's End*." In Olander and Greenberg, pp. 149–171.

Huntington, John. "From Man to Overmind: Arthur C. Clarke's Myth of Progress." In Olander and Greenberg, pp. 211–222.

Johnson, William, ed. *Focus on the Science Fiction Film*. Englewood Cliffs, New Jersey: Prentice-Hall, 1972.

Kagan, Norman. *The Cinema of Stanley Kubrick*. New York: Holt, Rinehart, and Winston, 1972.

Kozloff, Max. "*2001*." *Film Culture* 48–49 (1970), 53–56.

Leary, Daniel J. "The Ends of Childhood: Eschatology in Shaw and Clarke." *The Shaw Review* 16 (1973), 67–78.

Lehman-Wilzig, Sam N. "Science Fiction as Futurist Prediction: Alternative Visions of Heinlein and Clarke." *The Literary Review* 20 (1976), 133–151.

Lewis, C. S. *Of Other Worlds: Essays and Stories*. New York: Harcourt, Brace & World, 1967.

McConnell, Frank D. *The Spoken Seen: Film and the Romantic Imagination*. Baltimore: Johns Hopkins University Press, 1975.

Menger, Lucy. "The Appeal of *Childhood's End*." In *Critical Encounters: Writers and Themes in Science Fiction*, ed. by Dick Riley. New York: Frederick Ungar, 1978.

Moskowitz, Sam. *Seekers of Tomorrow*. Cleveland: World, 1966.

Moylan, Tom. "Ideological Contradiction in Clarke's *The City and the Stars*." *Science-Fiction Studies* 4 (1977), 150–157.

Mullen, R. D. "In Response to Mr. Astle." *Science-Fiction Studies* 5 (1978), 304–306.

Nedelkovich, Alexander. "The Stellar Parallels: Robert Silverberg, Larry Niven, and Arthur C. Clarke." *Extrapolation* 21 (1980), 348–360.

Olander, Joseph D., and Martin Harry Greenberg, eds. *Arthur C. Clarke.* New York: Taplinger, 1977.

Otten, Terry. "The Fallen and Evolving Worlds of *2001*." *Mosaic* 13 (Spring/Summer 1980), 41–50.

Parrinder, Patrick. *Science Fiction: A Critical Guide.* London: Longmans, 1979.

Phillips, Gene D. *Stanley Kubrick: A Film Odyssey.* New York: Popular Library, 1975.

Plank, Robert. "1001 Interpretations of *2001*." In Clareson's *SF: The Other Side of Realism*, pp. 265–267.

———. "Sons and Fathers in A.D. 2001." In Olander and Greenberg, pp. 121–148.

Rabkin, Eric S. *Arthur C. Clarke.* West Linn, Oregon: Starmont House, 1979; revised, 1980.

———. *The Fantastic in Literature.* Princeton, New Jersey: Princeton University Press, 1976.

Rogers, Robert. "The Psychology of the 'Double' in *2001*." *Hartford Studies in Literature* 1 (1969), 34–36.

Rose, Mark. *Alien Encounters.* Cambridge, Massachusetts: Harvard University Press, 1981.

Samuelson, David N. "*Childhood's End*: A Medium Stage of Adolescence?" In Olander and Greenberg, pp. 196–210.

Sanders, Scott. "The Disappearance of Character." In Parrinder, pp. 131–147.

Scholes, Robert, and Eric S. Rabkin. *Science Fiction.* New York: Oxford, 1977.

Slusser, George Edgar. *The Space Odysseys of Arthur C.*

Clarke. San Bernardino, California: The Borgo Press, 1978.

Stacy, Paul H. "Cinematic Thought." *Hartford Studies in Literature* 1 (1969), 124–130.

Stover, Leon E. "Apeman, Superman—or *2001*'s Answer to the World Riddle." In *Above the Human Landscape*, ed. by Leon E. Stover and Willis E. McNelly. Pacific Palisades, California: Goodyear, 1972.

Tanzy, Eugene. "Contrasting Views of Man and the Evolutionary Process: *Back to Methuselah* and *Childhood's End.*" In Olander and Greenberg, pp. 172–195.

Thompson, William Irwin. *At the Edge of History.* New York: Harper & Row, 1971.

Thron, E. Michael. "The Outsider from Inside: Clarke's Aliens." In Olander and Greenberg, pp. 72–86.

Walker, Alexander. *Stanley Kubrick Directs.* New York: Harcourt Brace Jovanovich, 1971.

Warrick, Patricia S. *The Cybernetic Imagination in Science Fiction.* Cambridge, Massachusetts: MIT, 1980.

Weinkauf, Mary S. "The Escape from the Garden." *The Texas Quarterly* 16 (1973), 66–72.

Wolfe, Gary K. "The Known and the Unknown: Structure and Image in Science Fiction." In Clareson's *Many Futures, Many Worlds*, pp. 94–116.

Wymer, Thomas L. "Perception and Value in Science Fiction." In Clareson's *Many Futures, Many Worlds*, pp. 1–13.